A problem well put is half-solved. The reactionary is a man of few words, well-chosen, which cut to the heart of a problem. In the history of ideas there have been works which have laid bare the problems of modernity, and whose elegance has pointed the way to their solution.

Imperium Press' Studies in Reaction series distills the essence of reactionary thought. The series presents in compact format those seminal works which need so few words to say so much about modernity.

Nick Land is an English philosopher, often described as the "father of accelerationism". Born in 1962, Land lectured on continental philosophy at the University of Warwick, where he co-founded the Cybernetic Culture Research Unit, a radically experimental interdisciplinary research body. One of the only explicitly right-wing academics to be described as "postmodern", Land was a formative influence on the neoreactionary movement of the late 2000s, and his extended series of articles titled *The Dark Enlightenment* captures the essence of that movement from his techno-futurist perspective.

THE DARK ENLIGHTENMENT

NICK LAND

PERTH
IMPERIUM PRESS
2023

Published by Imperium Press

www.imperiumpress.org

The Dark Enlightenment
published by Nick Land 2012

All rights are reserved. No part of this publication may be reproduced, stored in a retrieval system, or transmitted in any form or by any means, electronic, mechanical, photocopying, recording, or otherwise, without prior permission of Imperium Press. Enquiries concerning reproduction outside the scope of the above should be directed to Imperium Press.

FIRST EDITION

A catalogue record for this
book is available from the
National Library of Australia

ISBN 978-1-922602-68-8 Paperback
ISBN 978-1-922602-69-5 E-book

Imperium Press has no responsibility for the persistence or accuracy of URLs for external or third-party Internet websites referred to in this publication and does not guarantee that any content on such websites is, or will remain, accurate or appropriate.

CONTENTS

THE DARK ENLIGHTENMENT
  Introduction ... vii
  Note on the Text ... xiii
  Part 1: Neo-Reactionaries Head for the Exit ... 3
  Part 2: The Arc of History is Long, but it Bends towards Zombie Apocalypse ... 18
  Part 3: Untitled ... 32
  Part 4a: A Multi-Part Sub-Digression into Racial Terror ... 61
  Part 4b: Obnoxious Observations ... 76
  Part 4c: The Cracker Factory ... 95
  Part 4d: Odd Marriages ... 109
  Part 4e: Cross-Coded History ... 117
  Part 4f: Approaching the Bionic Horizon ... 128

Introduction

The Dark Enlightenment was composed as it was written, and initially published, in sequence, with only the slightest preliminary sense of direction. It managed, nevertheless, to deviate—almost immediately—even from this vague bearing. Thus, drifting off course from the start, it surrendered whatever prospect of theoretical integrity it might have had. If any systematicity remains to it, it is unmerited by its mode of production. Most probably, there is no such architectonic order to be found.

It is not the purpose of these new introductory remarks to repair a deficiency of coherent theoretical direction, which can scarcely elude the critical reader, or even the casual one. The aim, rather, is to contextualize *The Dark Enlightenment*, as it is, against a quite different text—wholly and inaccessibly virtual—which might have more successfully executed the intellectual task that the actual one set out upon.

The Dark Enlightenment, even in its new, specifically 'neoreactionary' sense, has—from the beginning—meant many things. Among these, however, priority belongs to the idea of an Enlightenment that was—if not missed—at least crucially eclipsed, and thus driven into the shadows, at first incidentally, but later programmatically. The primary concern of this abominated Enlightenment, which the West has since buried, was the elucidation of socio-historical *conservation laws*, found intolerable for their tragic structure, their pessimism, or darkness. The Dark Enlightenment is the resilient attachment to the ineluctable, and thus to fate, or providence. To identify it with an indiscriminate repudiation of the Enlightenment (or even Modernity) in general, therefore, has to be considered a mistake.

A conservation law annuls a specific narrative of progress. Every advance is—immediately, but elsewhere—complemented by a retreat. The philosophy of the market, as the Scottish Enlightenment gestated it, finds abundant evidence for such compensations, or as they would later be called, *perverse effects*. To generalize from John Gilmore's adage on the dynamics of the Internet, commercial processes interpret ethico-political interventions as damage, and route around them. Progressive domestication of the economy is illusory. The Austrian Economists that have preserved this insight into recent times were the critical lineage from which Neoreaction would be calved.

Two great thinkers of the socio-historical conservation law were to have been the twin pillars of The Dark Enlightenment. The mantra of Mencius Moldbug, *sovereignty is conserved*, considered as an invocation of the Hobbesian political philosophy, introduces the first of these. Thomas Hobbes determines the problem of power as strictly insoluble, in any terms that the later—and softer— Enlightenment could judge tolerable. A sovereign cannot be tamed, unless by a superior—and thus *real*—sovereignty. A monarch who can be overridden is a false king. The hidden king has to be sought elsewhere.

Introduction

Thus, mere political displacement masquerades as resolution, under the name of progress, as if power had been *dealt with*, rather than conveniently obscured.

The second progress-doubting Thomas, Malthus, is neglected both in the Neoreactionary writings of Mencius Moldbug, and in the *Dark Enlightenment* text. He was, however, to have provided its second structural pillar, under the rubric that selection, too, is conserved. The progressive softening of existence, no less than its liberation, is an illusion that can be sustained only by systematic inattention to iron mechanisms of compensation. Since *The Dark Enlightenment* was fatally distracted from this topic, there is perhaps slight cause to pursue it here.

The source of the distraction was the Trayvon Martin case, whose initial phases unfolded during the production of the text. This topic will no doubt be considered 'sensitive' even today. It will equally doubtless be generally accepted as unfortunate, but, crucially, for the emerging obstreperous right *in a trivial way*. The 'right'—what little at the time seemed to remain of it—consisted of those who could admit, first of all to themselves, that they did not much care about a random episode of criminality in one of America's many broken cities. It was an event that appeared primarily squalid. The concerted media campaign to make it mean something much more than this, something iconic, through which a moral lesson could be taught, led to a contemptuous *reaction* which, in this case, became self-propelling. Arguably, the decisive break in prevailing American political conventions occurred at this moment.

Propaganda is predominantly selection. Nothing so

crude as a lie is necessary to deviate massively from the truth. The left has long accepted a version of this argument, to the extent that it is limited to a critique of cultural canon construction. In its rightist application, it is directed primarily against journalism. It was the arbitrarily assumed right of the fourth estate *to decide what matters* that provoked an explosion of dissent. With this outbreak came the retrieval of Mencius Moldbug's analysis of 'the Cathedral'—or sovereign cultural establishment—within which epistemological and ecclesiastical functions had become entirely fused. It was against the Cathedral that the emerging, yet still at that time invisible, cultural-political counter-revolution would be waged.

The Trayvon Martin issue was, of course, a race issue, and it is by pushing back against Left race politics that the Dark Enlightenment becomes—and already in its genesis *became*—a scandal. If not exactly a discovery, the response to unapologetic Neoreaction was at least a stark confirmation of the fact that race occupies the central locus of *the sacred* in contemporary Occidental societies. There is no other topic upon which it is possible, with comparable nonchalance, to blaspheme. We find here the pre-eminent compilation of intolerable facts. This structure of sensitivity is itself an ethnographic peculiarity, still overwhelmingly dominant throughout the Western world order, and only there. The ideological excitement it generates is especially notable due to its ever-sharpening inconsistency with the conclusions of the genomically data-drenched natural sciences which the same civilization has unleashed. A vast collision between the basic scientific and religious inclinations of the Occident set the occasion for the

Introduction

Dark Enlightenment to re-surface. In this regard, we haven't seen anything yet.

Left race politics is most clearly enshrined in the principle of disparate impact, based upon the sacred assumption that demographic inequalities are *prima facie* evidence of systemic injustice. The Dark Enlightenment—as a concrete, contemporary cultural impulse—is defined by its rejection of this radically defective egalitarian-universalist syllogism. What it perceives instead is an empirical, and increasingly implausible, *egalitarian hypothesis* which has tended towards the preposterous as it has been substantialized. A strongly defensible presumption in favor of equal treatment has become a dogmatic denial of significant group differences, on no grounds other than those insisted upon by an ever-more explicit religious orthodoxy, with complementary coding of dissidence as heresy. If the Dark Enlightenment is to some considerable extent race obsessed, therefore, it is only—or at least primarily— reactively so. It refuses to consent to the dominant dogma that racially disproportionate social outcomes are definite signs of sin. Perhaps people are different (in multiple dimensions). Homogenous distribution throughout any social field is not a rational expectation, but a holy cause. *Racism*, like *Satan*, explains little. The basic proposal of Neoreaction, then, is deliberate desensitization to the drama of race, and its moral passion, combined with a skeptical openness to, and patience regarding, scientifically-honed evidence. The provocation of this stance has proven to be extreme.

In the age of Alt-Right racial fanaticism, the essentially liberal recommendation for a massively-hardened culture of neglect is easily misconstrued as a more positive commitment. Disentangling this confusion in an environment of incandescent political tension—and even collapse—is unlikely to be an easy thing. Fall-back to a genuinely liberal position is almost certainly unobtainable. If classical liberalism had been able to secure itself against mass politics–including mass race politics—Neoreaction would not have arisen from its grave.

Neoreaction coincides exactly with the expectation that democracy will die messily, as the popular degeneration of the liberal social order proceeds. The recent evolution of the Cathedral-guided democratic religion into populist nationalism provides no obvious grounds for the withdrawal of this prediction. This unblinking recognition of the Alt-Right as *something that had to come* is not an identification, however, but something far closer to the opposite. The Alt-Right is the Frankenstein monster progressivism has built. It is uniquely adapted to what *the people* have become in our time. Liberal failure has been succeeded by that of the left, and the Alt-Right has inherited the rotten remains. Nothing was surprising about this outcome, beside its precise schedule, and specific details.

The years now upon us look dark. It was all, already dark. At least now it is comparatively clear.

Nick Land.
March 2017.

Note on the Text

The Dark Enlightenment was not conceived of as a book, but a hypertext, a series of online articles or blog posts, and as such it does not perfectly lend itself to the format of a book. Some of the writing betrays this original format, as Land makes reference to future posts, as well as to obscure online personalities who are now unknown. Links in the original text have been footnoted—a number of them are now broken, private, or moved, and these are reflected in the footnotes. The text was supplied by the author himself as the best and most complete version available.

THE DARK ENLIGHTENMENT

Part 1: Neo-Reactionaries Head for the Exit

Enlightenment is not only a state, but an event, and a process. As the designation for an historical episode, concentrated in northern Europe during the 18th century, it is a leading candidate for the 'true name' of modernity, capturing its origin and essence ('Renaissance' and 'Industrial Revolution' are others). Between 'enlightenment' and 'progressive enlightenment' there is only an elusive difference, because illumination takes time—and feeds on itself, because enlightenment is self-confirming, its revelations 'self-evident', and because a retrograde, or reactionary, 'dark enlightenment' amounts almost to intrinsic contradiction. To become enlightened, in this historical sense, is to recognize, and then to pursue, a guiding light.

There were ages of darkness, and then enlightenment came. Clearly, advance has demonstrated itself, offering not only improvement, but also a model. Furthermore, unlike a renaissance, there is no need for an enlightenment to recall what was lost, or to emphasize the attractions of return. The elementary acknowledgement of enlightenment is already Whig history in miniature.

Once certain enlightened truths have been found self-evident, there can be no turning back, and conservatism is pre-emptively condemned—pre-destined—to paradox. F. A. Hayek, who refused to describe himself as a conservative, famously settled instead upon the term 'Old Whig', which—like 'classical liberal' (or the still more melancholy 'remnant')—accepts that progress isn't what it used to be. What could an Old Whig be, if not a reactionary progressive? And what on earth is that?

Of course, plenty of people already think they know what reactionary modernism looks like, and amidst the current collapse back into the 1930s their concerns are only likely to grow. Basically, it's what the 'F' word is for, at least in its progressive usage. A flight from democracy under these circumstances conforms so perfectly to expectations that it eludes specific recognition, appearing merely as an atavism, or confirmation of dire repetition.

Still, something is happening, and it is—at least in part—something else. One milestone was the April 2009 discussion hosted at Cato Unbound among libertarian thinkers (including Patri Friedman and Peter Thiel) in which disillusionment with the direction and possibilities of democratic politics was expressed with unusual forthrightness.[1] Thiel summarized the trend bluntly: "I no longer believe that freedom and democracy are compatible."[2]

---

[1] Patri Friedman et al, "From Scratch: Libertarian Institutions and Communities," Cato Unbound, April 2009, accessed August 05, 2022, https://www.cato-unbound.org/issues/april-2009/scratch-libertarian-institutions-communities/.

[2] Peter Thiel, "The Education of a Libertarian," Cato

Part 1: Neo-Reactionaries Head for the Exit

In August 2011, Michael Lind posted a democratic riposte at Salon, digging up some impressively malodorous dirt, and concluding:

> The dread of democracy by libertarians and classical liberals is justified. Libertarianism really is incompatible with democracy. Most libertarians have made it clear which of the two they prefer. The only question that remains to be settled is why anyone should pay attention to libertarians.[3]

Lind and the 'neo-reactionaries' seem to be in broad agreement that democracy is not only (or even) a *system*, but rather a *vector*, with an unmistakable direction. Democracy and 'progressive democracy' are synonymous, and indistinguishable from the expansion of the state. Whilst 'extreme right-wing' governments have, on rare occasions, momentarily arrested this process, its reversal lies beyond the bounds of democratic possibility. Since winning elections is overwhelmingly a matter of vote buying, and society's informational organs (education and media) are no more resistant to bribery than the electorate, a thrifty politician is simply an incompetent politician, and the democratic variant of Darwinism quickly eliminates such misfits from the gene pool. This is a reality that the left applauds, the establish-

Unbound, April 13, 2009, accessed August 02, 2022, https://www.cato-unbound.org/2009/04/13/peter-thiel/education-libertarian.
3 Michael Lind, "Why Libertarians Apologize for Autocracy," Salon, August 30, 2011, accessed August 02, 2022, http://www.salon.com/2011/08/30/lind_libertariansim/.

ment right grumpily accepts, and the libertarian right has ineffectively railed against. Increasingly, however, libertarians have ceased to care whether anyone is 'pay[ing them] attention'—they have been looking for something else entirely: an exit.

It is a structural inevitability that the libertarian voice is drowned out in democracy, and according to Lind it should be. Ever more libertarians are likely to agree. 'Voice' is democracy itself, in its historically dominant, Rousseauistic strain. It models the state as a representation of popular will, and making oneself heard means more politics. If voting as the mass self-expression of politically empowered peoples is a nightmare engulfing the world, adding to the hubbub doesn't help. Even more than Equality-vs-Liberty, Voice-vs-Exit is the rising alternative, and libertarians are opting for voiceless flight. Patri Friedman remarks: "we think that free exit is so important that we've called it the only Universal Human Right."[4]

For the hardcore neo-reactionaries, democracy is not merely doomed, it is doom itself. Fleeing it approaches an ultimate imperative. The subterranean current that propels such anti-politics is recognizably Hobbesian, a coherent dark enlightenment, devoid from its beginning of any Rousseauistic enthusiasm for popular expression. Predisposed, in any case, to perceive the politically awakened masses as a howling irrational mob, it conceives the dynamics of democratization as fundamentally degenerative: systematically consolidating and exacerbating private vices, resentments, and deficiencies until they

---

4 Referenced content no longer available.

Part 1: Neo-Reactionaries Head for the Exit

reach the level of collective criminality and comprehensive social corruption. The democratic politician and the electorate are bound together by a circuit of reciprocal incitement, in which each side drives the other to ever more shameless extremities of hooting, prancing cannibalism, until the only alternative to shouting is being eaten.

Where the progressive enlightenment sees political ideals, the dark enlightenment sees appetites. It accepts that governments are made out of people, and that they will eat well. Setting its expectations as low as reasonably possible, it seeks only to spare civilization from frenzied, ruinous, gluttonous debauch. From Thomas Hobbes to Hans-Hermann Hoppe and beyond, it asks: How can the sovereign power be prevented—or at least dissuaded—from devouring society? It consistently finds democratic 'solutions' to this problem risible, at best.

Hoppe advocates an anarcho-capitalist 'private law society', but between monarchy and democracy he does not hesitate (and his argument is strictly Hobbesian):

> As a hereditary monopolist, a king regards the territory and the people under his rule as his personal property and engages in the monopolistic exploitation of this "property." Under democracy, monopoly and monopolistic exploitation do not disappear. Rather, what happens is this: instead of a king and a nobility who regard the country as their private property, a temporary and interchangeable caretaker is put in monopolistic charge of the country. The caretaker does not own the country, but as long as he is

in office he is permitted to use it to his and his protégés' advantage. He owns its current use—usufruct—but not its capital stock. This does not eliminate exploitation. To the contrary, it makes exploitation less calculating and carried out with little or no regard to the capital stock. Exploitation becomes shortsighted and capital consumption will be systematically promoted.[5]

Political agents invested with transient authority by multi-party democratic systems have an overwhelming (and demonstrably irresistible) incentive to plunder society with the greatest possible rapidity and comprehensiveness. Anything they neglect to steal—or 'leave on the table'—is likely to be inherited by political successors who are not only unconnected, but actually opposed, and who can therefore be expected to utilize all available resources to the detriment of their foes. Whatever is left behind becomes a weapon in your enemy's hand. Best, then, to destroy what cannot be stolen. From the perspective of a democratic politician, any type of social good that is neither directly appropriable nor attributable to (their own) partisan policy is sheer waste, and counts for nothing, whilst even the most grievous social misfortune—so long as it can be assigned to

---

5 Hans-Hermann Hoppe & Anthony Wile, "Dr. Hans-Hermann Hoppe on the Impracticality of One-World Government and the Failure of Western-style Democracy," The Daily Bell, March 27, 2011, accessed August 02, 2022, https://www.thedailybell.com/all-articles/exclusive-interviews/anthony-wile-dr-hans-hermann-hoppe-on-the-impracticality-of-one-world-government-and-the-failure-of-western-style-democracy/.

a prior administration or postponed until a subsequent one—figures in rational calculations as an obvious blessing. The long-range techno-economic improvements and associated accumulation of cultural capital that constituted social progress in its old (Whig) sense are in nobody's political interest. Once democracy flourishes, they face the immediate threat of extinction.

Civilization, as a process, is indistinguishable from diminishing time-preference (or declining concern for the present in comparison to the future). Democracy, which both in theory and evident historical fact accentuates time-preference to the point of convulsive feeding-frenzy, is thus as close to a precise negation of civilization as anything could be, short of instantaneous social collapse into murderous barbarism or zombie apocalypse (which it eventually leads to). As the democratic virus burns through society, painstakingly accumulated habits and attitudes of forward-thinking, prudential, human and industrial investment, are replaced by a sterile, orgiastic consumerism, financial incontinence, and a 'reality television' political circus. Tomorrow might belong to the other team, so it's best to eat it all now.

Winston Churchill, who remarked in neo-reactionary style that "the best argument against democracy is a five-minute conversation with the average voter", is better known for suggesting "that democracy is the worst form of government except all the others that have been tried." Whilst never exactly conceding that "OK, democracy sucks (in fact, it *really* sucks), but what's the alternative?" the implication is obvious. The general tenor of this sensibility is attractive to modern conservatives, because it resonates with their wry, disillusioned acceptance of relentless civilizational deterioration, and with the associated intellectual apprehension of capitalism as an unappetizing but ineliminable default social arrangement, which remains after all catastrophic or merely impractical alternatives have been discarded. The market economy, on this understanding, is no more than a spontaneous survival strategy that stitches itself together amidst the ruins of a politically devastated world. Things will probably just get worse forever. So it goes.

So, what is the alternative? (There's certainly no point trawling through the 1930s for one.) "Can you imagine a 21st-century post-demotist society? One that saw itself as recovering from democracy, much as Eastern Europe sees itself as recovering from Communism?" asks supreme Sith Lord of the neo-reactionaries, Mencius Moldbug. "Well, I suppose that makes one of us."[6]

Moldbug's formative influences are Austro-libertarian, but that's all over. As he explains:

> […] libertarians cannot present a realistic picture of a world in which their battle gets won and stays won. They wind up looking for ways to push a world in which the State's natural downhill path is to grow, back up the hill. This prospect is Sisyphean, and it's understandable why it attracts so

---

6 Mencius Moldbug, "Against Political Freedom," Unqualified Reservations, August 16, 2007, accessed August 02, 2022, https://www.unqualified-reservations.org/2007/08/against-political-freedom/.

few supporters.[7]

His awakening into neo-reaction comes with the (Hobbesian) recognition that sovereignty cannot be eliminated, caged, or controlled. Anarcho-capitalist utopias can never condense out of science fiction, divided powers flow back together like a shattered Terminator, and constitutions have exactly as much real authority as a sovereign interpretative power allows them to have. The state isn't going anywhere because—to those who run it—it's worth far too much to give up, and as the concentrated instantiation of sovereignty in society, nobody can make it do anything. If the state cannot be eliminated, Moldbug argues, at least it can be cured of *democracy* (or systematic and degenerative bad government), and the way to do that is to *formalize* it. This is an approach he calls 'neo-cameralism'.

> To a neocameralist, a state is a business which owns a country. A state should be managed, like any other large business, by dividing logical ownership into negotiable shares, each of which yields a precise fraction of the state's profit. (A well-run state is very profitable.) Each share has one vote, and the shareholders elect a board, which hires and fires managers.
>
> This business's customers are its residents. A profitably-managed neocameralist state

[7] Mencius Moldbug, "Further Conversation on Regime Change," Unqualified Reservations, September 16, 2007, accessed August 02, 2022, https://www.unqualified-reservations.org/2007/09/further-conversation-on-regime-change/.

> will, like any business, serve its customers efficiently and effectively. Misgovernment equals mismanagement.[8]

Firstly, it is essential to squash the democratic myth that a state 'belongs' to the citizenry. The point of neo-cameralism is to buy out the real stakeholders in sovereign power, not to perpetuate sentimental lies about mass enfranchisement. Unless ownership of the state is formally transferred into the hands of its actual rulers, the neo-cameral transition will simply not take place, power will remain in the shadows, and the democratic farce will continue.

So, secondly, the ruling class must be plausibly identified. It should be noted immediately, in contradistinction to Marxist principles of social analysis, that this is not the 'capitalist bourgeoisie'. Logically, it cannot be. The power of the business class is already clearly formalized, in monetary terms, so the identification of capital with political power is perfectly redundant. It is necessary to ask, rather, *who do capitalists pay for political favors*, how much these favors are potentially worth, and how the authority to grant them is distributed. This requires, with a minimum of moral irritation, that the entire social landscape of political bribery ('lobbying') is exactly mapped, and the administrative, legislative, judicial, media, and academic privileges accessed by such bribes are converted into fungible shares. Insofar as voters are worth bribing, there is no need to entirely

---

8 Mencius Moldbug, "Against Political Freedom," Unqualified Reservations, August 16, 2007, accessed August 02, 2022, https://www.unqualified-reservations.org/2007/08/against-political-freedom/.

exclude them from this calculation, although their portion of sovereignty will be estimated with appropriate derision. The conclusion of this exercise is the mapping of a ruling entity that is the truly dominant instance of the democratic polity. Moldbug calls it the *Cathedral*.

The formalization of political powers, thirdly, allows for the possibility of effective government. Once the universe of democratic corruption is converted into a (freely transferable) shareholding in *gov-corp*, the owners of the state can initiate rational corporate governance, beginning with the appointment of a CEO. As with any business, the interests of the state are now precisely formalized as the maximization of long-term shareholder value. There is no longer any need for residents (clients) to take any interest in politics whatsoever. In fact, to do so would be to exhibit semi-criminal proclivities. If *gov-corp* doesn't deliver acceptable value for its taxes (sovereign rent), they can notify its customer service function, and if necessary take their custom elsewhere. *Gov-corp* would concentrate upon running an efficient, attractive, vital, clean, and secure country, of a kind that is able to draw customers. No voice, free exit.

> [...] although the full neocameralist approach has never been tried, its closest historical equivalents to this approach are the 18th-century tradition of enlightened absolutism as represented by Frederick the Great, and the 21st-century nondemocratic tradition as seen in lost fragments of the British Empire such as Hong Kong, Singapore and Dubai. These states appear to provide a very high quality of service to their

citizens, with no meaningful democracy at all. They have minimal crime and high levels of personal and economic freedom. They tend to be quite prosperous. They are weak only in political freedom, and political freedom is unimportant by definition when government is stable and effective.[9]

In European classical antiquity, democracy was recognized as a familiar phase of cyclical political development, fundamentally decadent in nature, and preliminary to a slide into tyranny. Today this classical understanding is thoroughly lost, and replaced by a global democratic ideology, entirely lacking in critical self-reflection, that is asserted not as a credible social-scientific thesis, or even as a spontaneous popular aspiration, but rather as a religious creed, of a specific, historically identifiable kind:

> [...] a received tradition I call Universalism, which is a nontheistic Christian sect. Some other current labels for this same tradition, more or less synonymous, are progressivism, multiculturalism, liberalism, humanism, leftism, political correctness, and the like. [...] Universalism is the dominant modern branch of Christianity on the Calvinist line, evolving from the English Dissenter or Puritan tradition through the Unitarian, Transcendentalist, and Progressive movements.

---

9 Mencius Moldbug, "How Dawkins got Pwned", Chapter 4, Unqualified Reservations, October 18, 2007, accessed August 02, 2022, https://www.unqualified-reservations.org/2007/10/how-dawkins-got-pwned-part-4/.

Part 1: Neo-Reactionaries Head for the Exit

> Its ancestral briar patch also includes a few sideways sprigs that are important enough to name but whose Christian ancestry is slightly better concealed, such as Rousseauvian laicism, Benthamite utilitarianism, Reformed Judaism, Comtean positivism, German Idealism, Marxist scientific socialism, Sartrean existentialism, Heideggerian postmodernism, etc, etc, etc. [...] Universalism, in my opinion, is best described as a *mystery cult of power*. [...] It's as hard to imagine Universalism without the State as malaria without the mosquito. [...] The point is that this thing, whatever you care to call it, is at least two hundred years old and probably more like five. It's basically the Reformation itself. [...] And just walking up to it and denouncing it as evil is about as likely to work as suing Shub-Niggurath in small-claims court.[10]

To comprehend the emergence of our contemporary predicament, characterized by relentless, totalizing[11] state expansion, the proliferation of spurious positive 'human rights' (claims on the resources of others backed by coercive bureaucracies), politicized money, reckless evangelical 'wars for democracy',[12] and

---

10   Ibid.
11   Paul Gottfried, "When Democracy Murders Liberty," Taki's Magazine, February 05, 2012, accessed August 02, 2022, https://www.takimag.com/article/when_democracy_murders_liberty/.
12   Justin Raimondo, "The 'Cairo 19' Got What they Deserve," Antiwar.com, February 10, 2012, accessed August   02,   2022,   https://original.antiwar.com/

comprehensive thought control arrayed in defense of universalistic dogma (accompanied by the degradation of science into a government public relations function), it is necessary to ask how Massachusetts came to conquer the world, as Moldbug does. With every year that passes, the international ideal of sound governance finds itself approximating more closely and rigidly to the standards set by the Grievance Studies departments of New England universities. This is the divine providence of the ranters and levelers, elevated to a planetary teleology, and consolidated as the reign of the Cathedral.

The Cathedral has substituted its gospel for everything we ever knew. Consider just the concerns expressed by America's founding fathers (compiled by 'Liberty-clinger', comment #1, here):

> *A democracy is nothing more than mob rule, where 51% of the people may take away the rights of the other 49%.*
> — Thomas Jefferson

> *Democracy is two wolves and a lamb voting on what to have for lunch. Liberty is a well-armed lamb contesting the vote!*
> — Benjamin Franklin[13]

> *Democracy never lasts long. It soon wastes, ex-*

justin/2012/02/09/the-cairo-19-got-what-they-deserve/.
13 Don't trust the attribution of the 'Benjamin Franklin' quote, above. According to Barry Popik, the saying was probably invented by James Bovard, in 1992. (Bovard remarks elsewhere: "There are few more dangerous errors in political thinking than to equate democracy with liberty.")

Part 1: Neo-Reactionaries Head for the Exit

hausts, and murders itself. There never was a democracy yet that did not commit suicide.
— John Adams

Democracies have ever been spectacles of turbulence and contention; have ever been found incompatible with personal security or the rights of property; and have in general been as short in their lives as they have been violent in their death.
— James Madison

We are a Republican Government. Real liberty is never found in despotism or in the extremes of democracy [...] it has been observed that a pure democracy if it were practicable would be the most perfect government. Experience has proved that no position is more false than this. The ancient democracies in which the people themselves deliberated never possessed one good feature of government. Their very character was tyranny [...]
— Alexander Hamilton

More on voting with your feet (and the incandescent genius of Moldbug), next...

Part 2:
The Arc of History is Long, but it Bends towards Zombie Apocalypse

> *It strikes me that if one is going to pursue this to its logical conclusion, the only way to have a genuinely democratic society would also be to abolish capitalism in this state.*
> — David Graeber

> *We can't have democracy with capitalism [...] Democracy and capitalism don't work together.*
> — Marina Sitrin[1]

> *That's always the trouble with history. It always looks like it's over. But it never is.*
> — Mencius Moldbug[2]

GOOGLING 'democracy' and 'liberty' together is highly enlightening, in a dark way. In cyberspace, at least,

---

[1] Both quotes found in: "Occupy Movement Wants to Abolish Capitalism," The College Fix, March 05, 2012, accessed August 03, 2022, https://www.thecollegefix.com/occupy-movement-wants-to-abolish-capitalism/.

[2] Quoted text is not in post linked, nor anywhere else in *Unqualified Reservations*.

it is clear that only a distinct minority think of these terms as positively coupled. If opinion is to be judged in terms of the Google spider and its digital prey, by far the most prevalent association is disjunctive, or antagonistic, drawing upon the reactionary insight that democracy poses a lethal menace to liberty, all but ensuring its eventual eradication. Democracy is to liberty as Gargantua to a pie ("Surely you can see that we love liberty, to the point of gut-rumbling and salivation…").

Steve H. Hanke lays out the case authoritatively in his short essay *On Democracy Versus Liberty*, focused upon the American experience:

> Most people, including most Americans, would be surprised to learn that the word "democracy" does not appear in the Declaration of Independence (1776) or the Constitution of the United States of America (1789). They would also be shocked to learn the reason for the absence of the word democracy in the founding documents of the U.S.A. Contrary to what propaganda has led the public to believe, America's Founding Fathers were skeptical and anxious about democracy. They were aware of the evils that accompany a tyranny of the majority. The Framers of the Constitution went to great lengths to ensure that the federal government was not based on the will of the majority and was not, therefore, democratic.
>
> If the Framers of the Constitution did not embrace democracy, what did they adhere to? To a man, the Framers agreed that the purpose of government was to secure citi-

zens in John Locke's trilogy of the rights to life, liberty and property.[3]

He elaborates:

> The Constitution is primarily a structural and procedural document that itemizes who is to exercise power and how they are to exercise it. A great deal of stress is placed on the separation of powers and the checks and balances in the system. These were not a Cartesian construct or formula aimed at social engineering, but a shield to protect the people from the government. In short, the Constitution was designed to govern the government, not the people.
>
> The Bill of Rights establishes the rights of the people against infringements by the State. The only thing that the citizens can demand from the State, under the Bill of Rights, is for a trial by a jury. The rest of the citizens' rights are protections from the State. For roughly a century after the Constitution was ratified, private property, contracts and free internal trade within the United States were sacred. The scope and scale of the government remained very constrained. All this was very consistent with what was understood to be liberty.[4]

As the spirit of reaction digs its Sith-tentacles into

---

3 Steve H. Hanke, "On Democracy Versus Liberty," Cato Institute, January 20, 2011, accessed August 03, 2022, https://www.cato.org/commentary/democracy-versus-liberty.
4 Ibid.

the brain, it becomes difficult to remember how the classical (or non-communist) progressive narrative could once have made sense. What were people thinking? What were they expecting from the emerging super-empowered, populist, cannibalistic state? Wasn't the eventual calamity entirely predictable? How was it ever possible to be a Whig?

The ideological credibility of radical democratization is not, of course, in question. As thinkers ranging from (Christian progressive) Walter Russell Mead to (atheistic reactionary) Mencius Moldbug have exhaustively detailed, it conforms so exactly to ultra-protestant religious enthusiasm that its power to animate the revolutionary soul should surprise nobody. Within just a few years of Martin Luther's challenge to the papal establishment, peasant insurrectionists were stringing up their class enemies all over Germany.

The empirical credibility of democratic advancement is far more perplexing, and also genuinely complex (which is to say controversial, or more precisely, worthy of a data-based, rigorously-argued controversy). In part, that is because the modern configuration of democracy emerges within the sweep of a far broader modernistic trend, whose techno-scientific, economic, social and political strands are obscurely interrelated, knitted together by misleading correlations, and subsequent false causalities. If, as Schumpeter argues, industrial capitalism tends to engender a democratic-bureaucratic culture that concludes in stagnation, it might nevertheless seem as though democracy was 'associated' with material progress. It is easy to misconstrue a lagging indicator as a positive causal factor, especially when ideological zeal lends its bias to the misapprehension. In similar vein, since cancer only afflicts living beings, it might—with apparent reason—be associated with vitality.

Robin Hanson (gently) notes:

> Yes many trends have been positive for a century or so, and yes this suggests they will continue to rise for a century or so. But no this does not mean that students are empirically or morally wrong for thinking it "utopian fantasy" that one could "end poverty, disease, tyranny, and war" by joining a modern-day Kennedy's political quest. Why? Because positive recent trends in these areas were not much caused by such political movements! They were mostly caused by our getting rich from the industrial revolution, an event that political movements tended, if anything, to try to hold back on average.[5]

Simple historical chronology suggests that industrialization supports progressive democratization, rather than being derived from it. This observation has even given rise to a widely accepted school of pop social science theorizing, according to which the 'maturation' of societies in a democratic direction is determined by thresholds of affluence, or middle-class formation. The strict logical correlate of such ideas, that democracy is *fundamentally non-productive* in relation to material progress, is typically

---

5 Robin Hanson, "Is Pessimism Immoral?", overcoming bias, February 27, 2012, accessed August 03, 2022, https://www.overcomingbias.com/2012/02/is-pessimism-immoral.html.

under-emphasized. Democracy *consumes* progress. When perceived from the perspective of the dark enlightenment, the appropriate mode of analysis for studying the democratic phenomenon is general parasitology.

Quasi-libertarian responses to the outbreak accept this implicitly. Given a population deeply infected by the zombie virus and shambling into cannibalistic social collapse, the preferred option is quarantine. It is not communicative isolation that is essential, but a functional dis-solidarization of society that tightens feedback loops and exposes people with maximum intensity to the consequences of their own actions. Social solidarity, in precise contrast, is the parasite's friend. By cropping out all high-frequency feedback mechanisms (such as market signals), and replacing them with sluggish, infra-red loops that pass through a centralized forum of 'general will', a radically democratized society insulates parasitism from what it does, transforming local, painfully dysfunctional, intolerable, and thus urgently corrected behavior patterns into global, numbed, and chronic socio-political pathologies.

Gnaw off other people's body parts and it might be hard to get a job—that's the kind of lesson a tight-feedback, cybernetically intense, laissez faire order would allow to be learned. It's also exactly the kind of insensitive zombiephobic discrimination that any compassionate democracy would denounce as thought crime, whilst boosting the public budget for the vitally-challenged, undertaking consciousness raising campaigns on behalf of those suffering from involuntary cannibalistic impulse syndrome, affirming the dignity of the zombie lifestyle in higher-education curriculums, and rigorously regulating workspaces to ensure that the shuffling undead are not victimized by profit-obsessed, performance-centric, or even unreconstructed animationist employers.

As enlightened zombie-tolerance flourishes in the shelter of the democratic mega-parasite, a small remnant of reactionaries, attentive to the effects of real incentives, raise the formulaic question: "You do realize that these policies lead inevitably to a massive expansion of the zombie population?" The dominant vector of history presupposes that such nuisance objections are marginalized, ignored, and—wherever possible—silenced through social ostracism. The remnant either fortifies the basement, whilst stocking up on dried food, ammunition, and silver coins, or accelerates the application process for a second passport, and starts packing its bags.

If all of this seems to be coming unmoored from historical concreteness, there's a conveniently topical remedy: a little digressive channel-hopping over to Greece. As a microcosmic model for the death of the West, playing out in real time, the Greek story is hypnotic. It describes a 2,500-year arc that is far from neat, but irresistibly dramatic, from proto-democracy to accomplished zombie apocalypse. Its pre-eminent virtue is that it perfectly illustrates the democratic mechanism *in extremis*, separating individuals and local populations from the consequences of their decisions by scrambling their behavior through large-scale, centralized re-distribution systems. You decide what you do, but then vote on the consequences. How could anyone say 'no' to that?

No surprise that over 30 years of EU membership Greeks have been eagerly cooperating with a social-engineering mega-project that strips out all short-wave social signals and re-routes feedback through the grandiose circuitry of European solidarity, ensuring that all economically-relevant information is red-shifted through the heat-death sump of the European Central Bank.[6] Most specifically, it has conspired with 'Europe' to obliterate all information that might be contained in Greek interest rates, thus effectively disabling all financial feedback on domestic policy choices.

This is democracy in a consummate form that defies further perfection, since nothing conforms more exactly to the 'general will' than the legislative abolition of reality, and nothing delivers the hemlock to reality more definitively than the coupling of Teutonic interest rates with East Mediterranean spending decisions. Live like Hellenes and pay like Germans—any political party that failed to rise to power on that platform deserves to scrabble for vulture-picked scraps in the wilderness. It's the ultimate no-brainer, in just about every imaginable sense of that expression. What could possibly go wrong?

More to the point, what did go wrong? Mencius Moldbug begins his *Unqualified Reservations* series *How Dawkins Got Pwned* (or taken over through an "exploitable vulnerability") with the outlining of design rules for a hypothetical "optimal memetic parasite" that would be "as virulent as possible. It

---

6 "Ex-ECB's Juergen Stark Says ECB's Balance Sheet 'Gigantic', Collateral Quality 'Shocking'," ZeroHedge, March 08, 2012, accessed August 03, 2022, https://www.zerohedge.com/news/ex-ecbs-juergen-stark-says-ecbs-balance-sheet-gigantic-collateral-quality-shocking.

will be highly contagious, highly morbid, and highly persistent. A really ugly bug."[7] In comparison to this ideological super-plague, the vestigial monotheism derided in *The God Delusion* would figure as nothing worse than a moderately unpleasant head cold. What begins as abstract meme tinkering concludes as grand-sweep history, in the dark enlightenment mode:

> My belief is that Professor Dawkins is not just a Christian atheist. He is a *Protestant atheist*. And he is not just a Protestant atheist. He is a *Calvinist atheist*. And he is not just a Calvinist atheist. He is an *Anglo-Calvinist atheist*. In other words, he can be also described as a Puritan atheist, a Dissenter atheist, a Nonconformist atheist, an Evangelical atheist, etc, etc.
>
> This cladistic taxonomy traces Professor Dawkins' intellectual ancestry back about 400 years, to the era of the English Civil War. Except of course for the atheism theme, Professor Dawkins' kernel is a remarkable match for the Ranter, Leveller, Digger, Quaker, Fifth Monarchist, or any of the more extreme English Dissenter traditions that flourished during the Cromwellian interregnum.
>
> Frankly, these dudes were freaks. Maniacal fanatics. Any mainstream English thinker

---

[7] Mencius Moldbug, "How Dawkins got Pwned," Chapter 1, Unqualified Reservations, September 26, 2007, accessed August 03, 2022, https://www.unqualified-reservations.org/2007/09/how-dawkins-got-pwned-part-1/.

of the 17th, 18th or 19th century, informed that this tradition (or its modern descendant) is now the planet's dominant Christian denomination, would regard this as a sign of imminent apocalypse. If you're sure they're wrong, you're more sure than me.

Fortunately, Cromwell himself was comparatively moderate. The extreme ultra-Puritan sects never got a solid lock on power under the Protectorate. Even more fortunately, Cromwell got old and died, and Cromwellism died with him. Lawful government was restored to Great Britain, as was the Church of England, and Dissenters became a marginal fringe again. And frankly, a damned good riddance it was.

However, you can't keep a good parasite down. A community of Puritans fled to America and founded the theocratic colonies of New England. After its military victories in the American Rebellion and the War of Secession, American Puritanism was well on the way to world domination. Its victories in World War I, World War II, and the Cold War confirmed its global hegemony. All legitimate mainstream thought on Earth today is descended from the American Puritans, and through them the English Dissenters.[8]

---

8 Mencius Moldbug, "How Dawkins got Pwned," Chapter 2, Unqualified Reservations, October 04, 2007, accessed August 03, 2022, https://www.unqualified-reservations.org/2007/10/how-dawkins-got-pwned-part-2/.

Given the rise of this "really ugly bug" to world dominion, it might seem strange to pick on a tangential figure such as Dawkins, but Moldbug selects his target for exquisitely-judged strategic reasons. Moldbug identifies with Dawkins' Darwinism, with his intellectual repudiation of Abrahamic theism, and with his broad commitment to scientific rationality. Yet he recognizes, crucially, that Dawkins' critical faculties shut off—abruptly and often comically—at the point where they might endanger a still broader commitment to hegemonic progressivism. In this way, Dawkins is powerfully indicative. Militant secularism is itself a modernized variant of the Abrahamic meta-meme, on its Anglo-Protestant, radical democratic taxonomic branch, *whose specific tradition is anti-traditionalism.* The clamorous atheism of *The God Delusion* represents a protective feint, and a consistent upgrade of religious reformation, guided by a spirit of progressive enthusiasm that trumps empiricism and reason, whilst exemplifying an irritable dogmatism that rivals anything to be found in earlier God-themed strains.

Dawkins isn't merely an enlightened modern progressive and implicit radical democrat, he's an impressively credentialed scientist, more specifically a biologist, and (thus) a Darwinian evolutionist. The point at which he touches the limit of acceptable thinking as defined by the memetic super-bug is therefore quite easy to anticipate. His inherited tradition of low-church ultra-protestantism has replaced God with Man as the locus of spiritual investment, and 'Man' has been in the process of Darwinian research dissolution for over 150 years. (As the sound, decent person I know you are, having gotten this far with Moldbug you're probably already muttering under your breath, *don't mention race, don't mention race, don't mention race, please, oh please, in the name of the Zeitgeist and the dear sweet non-god of progress, don't mention race …*) … but Moldbug is already[9] citing Dawkins, citing Thomas Huxley "[…] in a contest which is to be carried out by thoughts and not by bites. The highest places in the hierarchy of civilization will assuredly not be within the reach of our dusky cousins." Which Dawkins frames by remarking: "Had Huxley […] been born and educated in our time, [he] would have been the first to cringe with us at [his] Victorian sentiments and unctuous tone. I quote them only to illustrate how the *Zeitgeist* moves on."

It gets worse. Moldbug seems to be holding Huxley's hand, and … (ewww!) doing that palm-stroking thing with his finger. This sure ain't vanilla-libertarian reaction anymore—it's getting seriously dark, and scary. "In all seriousness, what is the evidence for fraternism? Why, exactly, does Professor Dawkins believe that all neohominids are born with identical potential for neurological development? He doesn't say. Perhaps he thinks it's obvious."[10]

Whatever one's opinion on the respective scientific merits of human biological diversity or uniformity, it is surely beyond contention that the latter assumption, alone, is *tolerated*. Even if progressive-univer-

---

9 Mencius Moldbug, "How Dawkins got Pwned," Chapter 3, Unqualified Reservations, October 11, 2007, accessed August 03, 2022, https://www.unqualified-reservations.org/2007/10/how-dawkins-got-pwned-part-3/.
10 Ibid.

salistic beliefs about human nature are true, they are not held because they are true, or arrived at through any process that passes the laugh test for critical scientific rationality. They are received as religious tenets, with all of the passionate intensity that characterizes essential items of faith, and to question them is not a matter of scientific inaccuracy, but of what we now call *political incorrectness*, and once knew as *heresy*.

To sustain this transcendent moral posture in relation to *racism* is no more rational than subscription to the doctrine of *original sin*, of which it is, in any case, the unmistakable modern substitute. The difference, of course, is that 'original sin' is a traditional doctrine, subscribed to by an embattled social cohort, significantly under-represented among public intellectuals and media figures, deeply unfashionable in the dominant world culture, and widely criticized—if not derided—without any immediate assumption that the critic is advocating murder, theft, or adultery. To question the status of racism as the supreme and defining social sin, on the other hand, is to court universal condemnation from social elites, and to arouse suspicions of *thought crimes* that range from pro-slavery apologetics to genocide fantasies. Racism is *pure or absolute evil*, whose proper sphere is the infinite and the eternal, or the incendiary sinful depths of the hyper-protestant soul, rather than the mundane confines of civil interaction, social scientific realism, or efficient and proportional legality. The dissymmetry of affect, sanction, and raw social power attending old heresies and their replacements, once noticed, is a nagging indicator. A new sect reigns, and it is not even especially well hidden.

Part 2: The Arc of History is Long

Yet even among the most hardened HBD constituencies, hysterical sanctification of plus-good race-think hardly suffices to lend radical democracy the aura of profound morbidity that Moldbug detects. That requires a devotional relation to the State.

Part 3:
Untitled

THE previous installment of this series ended with our hero Mencius Moldbug, up to his waist (or worse) in the mephitic swamp of political incorrectness, approaching the dark heart of his politico-religious meditation on *How Dawkins Got Pwned*. Moldbug has caught Dawkins in the midst of a symptomatically significant, and excruciatingly sanctimonious, denunciation of Thomas Huxley's racist "Victorian sentiments"—a sermon which concludes with the strange declaration that he is quoting Huxley's words, despite their self-evident and wholly intolerable ghastliness, "only to illustrate how the *Zeitgeist* moves on."

Moldbug pounces, asking pointedly: "What, exactly, is this Zeitgeist thing?" It is, indisputably, an extraordinary catch. Here is a thinker (Dawkins), trained as a biologist, and especially fascinated by the (disjunctively) twinned topics of naturalistic evolution and Abrahamic religion, stumbling upon what he apprehends as a one-way trend of world-historical spiritual development, which he then—emphatically, but without the slightest appeal to disciplined reason or evidence—denies has any serious connection to the advance of science, human biology, or religious tradition. The stammering nonsense that results is a thing of wonder, but for Moldbug it all makes sense:

> In fact, Professor Dawkins' *Zeitgeist* is […] indistinguishable from […] the old Anglo-Calvinist or Puritan concept of *Providence*. Perhaps this is a false match. But it's quite a close one.
>
> Another word for *Zeitgeist* is *Progress*. It's unsurprising that Universalists tend to believe in Progress—in fact, in a political context, they often call themselves *progressives*. Universalism has indeed made quite a bit of progress since [the time of Huxley's embarrassing remark in] 1913. But this hardly refutes the proposition that Universalism is a parasitic tradition. Progress for the tick is not progress for the dog.[1]

What, exactly, is this *Zeitgeist* thing? The question bears repeating. Is it not astounding, to begin with, that when one English Darwinian reaches for a weapon to club another, the most convenient cudgel to hand should be a German word—associated with an abstruse lineage of state-worshipping idealistic philosophy—explicitly referencing a conception of historical time that has no discernible connection to the process of naturalistic evolution? It is as if, scarcely imaginably, during a comparable contention

---

1 Mencius Moldbug, "How Dawkins got Pwned," Chapter 3, Unqualified Reservations, October 11, 2007, accessed August 03, 2022, https://www.unqualified-reservations.org/2007/10/how-dawkins-got-pwned-part-3/.

among physicists (on the topic of quantum indeterminacy), one should suddenly hear it shouted that "God does not play dice with the universe." In fact, the two examples are intimately entangled, since Dawkins' faith in the *Zeitgeist* is combined with adherence to the dogmatic progressivism of 'Einsteinian Religion' (meticulously dissected,[2] of course, by Moldbug).

The shamelessness is remarkable, or at least it would be, were it naively believed that the protocols of scientific rationality occupied the sovereign position in such disputation, if only in principle. In fact—and here irony is amplified to the very brink of howling psychosis—Einstein's Old One still reigns. The criteria of judgment owe everything to neo-puritan spiritual hygiene, and nothing whatsoever to testable reality. Scientific utterance is screened for conformity to a progressive social agenda, whose authority seems to be unaffected by its complete indifference to scientific integrity. It reminds Moldbug of Lysenko, for understandable reasons.

"If the facts do not agree with the theory, so much worse for the facts" Hegel asserted. It is the *Zeitgeist* that is God, historically incarnated in the state, trampling mere data back into the dirt. By now, everybody knows where this ends. An egalitarian moral ideal, hardened into a universal axiom or increasingly incontestable dogma, completes modernity's supreme historical irony by making 'tolerance' the

---

[2] Mencius Moldbug, "How Dawkins got Pwned," Chapter 1, Unqualified Reservations, September 26, 2007, accessed August 03, 2022, https://www.unqualified-reservations.org/2007/09/how-dawkins-got-pwned-part-1/.

iron criterion for the limits of (cultural) toleration. Once it is accepted universally, or, speaking more practically, by all social forces wielding significant cultural power, that *intolerance is intolerable*, political authority has legitimated anything and everything convenient to itself, without restraint.

That is the magic of the dialectic, or of logical perversity. When only *tolerance is tolerable*, and everyone (who matters) accepts this manifestly nonsensical formula as not only rationally intelligible, but as the universally-affirmed principle of modern democratic faith, nothing except politics remains. Perfect tolerance and absolute intolerance have become logically indistinguishable, with either equally interpretable as the other, A = not-A, or the inverse, and in the nakedly Orwellian world that results, power alone holds the keys of articulation. Tolerance has progressed to such a degree that it has become a social police function, providing the existential pretext for new inquisitional institutions. ("We must remember that those who tolerate intolerance abuse tolerance itself, and an enemy of tolerance is an enemy of democracy," Moldbug ironizes.)[3]

The spontaneous tolerance that characterized classical liberalism, rooted in a modest set of strictly negative rights that restricted the domain of politics, or government intolerance, surrenders during the democratic surge-tide to a positive *right to be tolerated*, defined ever more expansively as substantial entitlement, encompassing public affirmations

---

3 Mencius Moldbug, "Petition Against the Reactosphere," Unqualified Reservations, July 31, 2011, accessed August 03, 2022, https://www.unqualified-reservations.org/2011/07/petition-against-reactosphere/.

of dignity, state-enforced guarantees of equal treatment by all agents (public and private), government protections against non-physical slights and humiliations, economic subsidies, and—ultimately—statistically proportional representation within all fields of employment, achievement, and recognition. That the eschatological culmination of this trend is simply impossible matters not at all to the dialectic. On the contrary, it energizes the political process, combusting any threat of policy satiation in the fuel of infinite grievance. "I will not cease from Mental Fight, Nor shall my Sword sleep in my hand: Till we have built Jerusalem, In England's green and pleasant land." Somewhere before Jerusalem is reached, the inarticulate pluralism of a free society has been transformed into the assertive multiculturalism of a soft-totalitarian democracy.

The Jews of 17th-century Amsterdam, or the Huguenots of 18th-century London, enjoyed the right to be left alone, and enriched their host societies in return. The democratically-empowered grievance groups of later modern times are incited by political leaders to demand a (fundamentally illiberal) *right to be heard*, with social consequences that are predominantly malignant. For politicians, however, who identify and promote themselves as the voice of the unheard and the ignored, the self-interest at stake could hardly be more obvious.

Tolerance, which once presupposed neglect, now decries it, and in so doing becomes its opposite. Were this a partisan development, partisan politics of a democratic kind might sustain the possibility of reversion, but it is nothing of the kind. 'When someone is hurting, government has got to move' declared 'compassionate conservative' US President George W. Bush, in a futile effort to channel the Cathedral. When the 'right' sounds like this it is not only dead, but unmistakably reeking of advanced decomposition. 'Progress' has won, but is that bad? Moldbug approaches the question rigorously:

> If a tradition causes its hosts to make miscalculations that compromise their personal goals, it exhibits Misesian morbidity. If it causes its hosts to act in ways that compromise their genes' reproductive interests, it exhibits Darwinian morbidity. If subscribing to the tradition is individually advantageous or neutral (defectors are rewarded, or at least unpunished) but collectively harmful, the tradition is parasitic. If subscribing is individually disadvantageous but collectively beneficial, the tradition is altruistic. If it is both individually and collectively benign, it is symbiotic. If it is both individually and collectively harmful, it is malignant. Each of these labels can be applied to either Misesian or Darwinian morbidity. A theme that is arational, but does not exhibit either Misesian or Darwinian morbidity, is trivially morbid.[4]

Behaviorally considered, the Misesian and Darwinian systems are clusters of 'selfish' incentives,

---

4 Mencius Moldbug, "How Dawkins got Pwned," Chapter 2, Unqualified Reservations, October 04, 2007, accessed August 03, 2022, https://www.unqualifiedreservations.org/2007/10/how-dawkins-got-pwned-part-2/.

oriented respectively to property accumulation and gene propagation. Whilst the Darwinians conceive the 'Misesian' sphere as a special case of genetically self-interested motivation, the Austrian tradition, rooted in highly rationalized neo-kantian anti-naturalism, is pre-disposed to resist such reductionism. Whilst the ultimate implications of this contest are considerable, under current conditions it is a squabble of minor urgency, since both formations are united in 'hate', which is to say, in their reactionary tolerance for incentive structures that punish the maladapted.

'Hate' is a word to pause over. It testifies with special clarity to the religious orthodoxy of the Cathedral, and its peculiarities merit careful notice. Perhaps its most remarkable feature is its perfect redundancy, when evaluated from the perspective of any analysis of legal and cultural norms that is not enflamed by neo-puritan evangelical enthusiasm. A 'hate crime', if it is anything at all, is just a crime, plus 'hate', and what the 'hate' adds is telling. To restrict ourselves, momentarily, to examples of uncontroversial criminality, one might ask: what is it exactly that aggravates a murder, or assault, if the motivation is attributed to 'hate'? Two factors seem especially prominent, and neither has any obvious connection to common legal norms.

Firstly, the crime is augmented by a purely ideational, ideological, or even 'spiritual' element, attesting not only to a violation of civilized conduct, but also to a heretical intention. This facilitates the complete abstraction of hate from criminality, whereupon it takes the form of 'hate-speech' or simply 'hate' (which is always to be contrasted with the 'passion', 'outrage', or righteous 'anger' represented by critical, controversial, or merely abusive language directed against unprotected groups, social categories, or individuals). 'Hate' is an offense against the Cathedral itself, a refusal of its spiritual guidance, and a mental act of defiance against the manifest religious destiny of the world.

Secondly, and relatedly, 'hate' is deliberately and even strategically asymmetrical in respect to the equilibrium political polarity of advanced democratic societies. Between the relentless march of progress and the ineffective grouching of conservatism it does not vacillate. As we have seen, only the right can 'hate'. As the doxological immunity system of 'hate' suppression is consolidated within elite educational and media systems, the highly selective distribution of protections ensures that 'discourse'—especially empowered discourse—is ratcheted consistently to the left, which is to say, in the direction of an ever more comprehensively radicalized Universalism. The morbidity of this trend is extreme.

Because grievance status is awarded as political compensation for economic incompetence, it constructs an automatic cultural mechanism that advocates for dysfunction. The Universalist creed, with its reflex identification of inequality with injustice, can conceive no alternative to the proposition that the lower one's situation or status, the more compelling is one's claim upon society, the purer and nobler one's cause. Temporal failure is the sign of spiritual election (Marxo-Calvinism), and to dispute any of this is clearly 'hate'.

This does not compel even the most hard-hearted neo-reactionary to suggest, in a caricature of the high Victorian cultural style, that social disadvantage, as manifested in political violence, criminality, homelessness, insolvency, and welfare dependency, is a simple index of moral culpability. In large part—perhaps overwhelmingly large part—it reflects sheer misfortune. Dim, impulsive, unhealthy, and unattractive people, reared chaotically in abusive families, and stranded in broken, crime-wracked communities, have every reason to curse the gods before themselves. Besides, disaster can strike anyone.

In regards to effective incentive structures, however, none of this is of the slightest importance. Behavioral reality knows only one iron law: **Whatever is subsidized is promoted**. With a necessity no weaker than that of entropy itself, insofar as social democracy seeks to soften bad consequences—for major corporations no less than for struggling individuals or hapless cultures—things get worse. There is no way around, or beyond this formula, only wishful thinking, and complicity with degeneration. Of course, this defining reactionary insight is doomed to inconsequence, since it amounts to the supremely unpalatable conclusion that every attempt at 'progressive' improvement is fated to reverse itself, 'perversely', into horrible failure. No democracy could accept this, which means that every democracy will fail.

The excited spiral of Misesian-Darwinian degenerative runaway is neatly captured in the words of the world's fluffiest Beltway libertarian, Megan McArdle, writing in core Cathedral-mouthpiece *The Atlantic*:

> It is somewhat ironic that the first serious strains caused by Europe's changing demo-

graphics are showing up in the Continent's welfare budgets, because the pension systems themselves may well have shaped, and limited, Europe's growth. The 20th century saw international adoption of social-security systems that promised defined benefits paid out of future tax revenue—known to pension experts as "paygo" systems, and to critics as Ponzi schemes. These systems have greatly eased fears of a destitute old age, but multiple studies show that as social-security systems become more generous (and old age more secure), people have fewer children. By one estimate, 50 to 60 percent of the difference between America's (above-replacement) birthrate and Europe's can be explained by the latter's more generous systems. In other words, Europe's pension system may have set in motion the very demographic decline that helped make that system—and some European governments—insolvent.[5]

Despite McArdle's ridiculous suggestion that the United States of America has in some way exempted itself from Europe's mortuary path, the broad outline of the diagnosis is clear, and increasingly accepted as commonsensical (although best ignored). According to the rising creed, welfare attained through progeny and savings is non-universal, and thus morally-benighted. It should be supplanted, as widely and

---

5 Megan McArdle, "Europe's Real Crisis," The Atlantic, April 2012, accessed August 03, 2022, https://www.theatlantic.com/magazine/archive/2012/04/europes-real-crisis/308915/.

rapidly as possible, by universal benefits or 'positive rights' distributed universally to the democratic citizen and thus, inevitably, routed through the altruistic State. If as a result, due to the irredeemable political incorrectness of reality, economies and populations should collapse in concert, at least it will not damage our souls. Oh democracy! You saccharine-sweet dying idiot, what do you think the zombie hordes will care for your soul?

Moldbug comments:

> Universalism, in my opinion, is best described as a mystery cult of power.
>
> It's a cult of power because one critical stage in its replicative lifecycle is a little critter called the State. When we look at the big U's surface proteins, we notice that most of them can be explained by its need to capture, retain, and maintain the State, and direct its powers toward the creation of conditions that favor the continued replication of Universalism. It's as hard to imagine Universalism without the State as malaria without the mosquito.
>
> It's a mystery cult because it displaces theistic traditions by replacing metaphysical superstitions with philosophical mysteries, such as humanity, progress, equality, democracy, justice, environment, community, peace, etc.
>
> None of these concepts, as defined in orthodox Universalist doctrine, is even slightly coherent. All can absorb arbitrary mental energy without producing any rational thought. In this they are best compared to Plotinian, Talmudic, or Scholastic non-

sense.[6]

As a bonus, here's the Urban Feature guide to the main sequence of modern political regimes:

> **Regime (1)**: Communist Tyranny
> **Typical Growth:** ~0%
> **Voice/Exit:** Low/Low
> **Cultural climate:** Psychotic utopianism
> **Life is ...** hard but 'fair'
> **Transition Mechanism:** Re-discovers markets at economic degree-zero
>
> **Regime (2):** Authoritarian Capitalism
> **Typical Growth:** 5–10%
> **Voice/Exit:** Low/High
> **Cultural Climate:** Flinty realism
> **Life is ...** hard but productive
> **Transition Mechanism:** Pressurized by the Cathedral to democratize
>
> **Regime (3):** Social Democracy
> **Typical Growth:** 0–3%
> **Voice/Exit:** High/High
> **Cultural Climate:** Sanctimonious dishonesty
> **Life is ...** soft and unsustainable
> **Transition Mechanism:** Can-kicking runs out of road
>
> **Regime (4):** Zombie Apocalypse

---

6 Mencius Moldbug, "How Dawkins got Pwned," Chapter 3, Unqualified Reservations, October 11, 2007, accessed August 03, 2022, https://www.unqualified-reservations.org/2007/10/how-dawkins-got-pwned-part-3/.

Land

Typical Growth: N/A
Voice/Exit: High (mostly useless screaming)/High (with fuel, ammo, dried food, precious metal coins)
Cultural Climate: Survivalism
Life is ... hard-to-impossible
Transition Mechanism: Unknown

For all regimes, growth expectations assume moderately competent population, otherwise go straight to (4).

Part 4:
Re-Running the Race to Ruin

Liberals are baffled and infuriated that poor whites vote Republican, yet voting on tribal grounds is a feature of all multi-ethnic democracies, whether [in] Northern Ireland, Lebanon or Iraq. The more a majority becomes a minority the more tribal its voting becomes, so that increasingly the Republicans have become the "white party"; making this point indelicately got Pat Buchanan the sack, but many others make it too.

Will it happen here [in the UK]? The patterns are not dissimilar. In the 2010 election the Conservatives won only 16 per cent of the ethnic minority vote, while Labour won the support of 72 per cent of Bangladeshis, 78 per cent of African-Caribbeans and 87 per cent of Africans. The Tories are slightly stronger among British Hindus and Sikhs—mirroring Republican support among Asian-Americans—who are more likely to be home-owning professionals and feel less alienated.

The Economist recently asked if the Tories had a "race problem", but it may just be that democracy has a race problem.[1]

1 Content unavailable.

Land

— Ed West

Without a taste for irony, Mencius Moldbug is all but unendurable, and certainly unintelligible. Vast structures of historical irony shape his writings, at times even engulfing them. How otherwise could a proponent of traditional configurations of social order—a self-proclaimed Jacobite—compose a body of work that is stubbornly dedicated to subversion?

Irony is Moldbug's method, as well as his milieu. This can be seen, most tellingly, in his chosen name for the usurped enlightenment, the dominant faith of the modern world: Universalism. This is a word that he appropriates (and capitalizes) within a reactionary diagnosis whose entire force lies in its exposure of an exorbitant particularity.

Moldbug turns continually to history (or, more rigorously, *cladistics*), to accurately specify that which asserts its own universal significance whilst ascending to a state of general dominance that approaches the universal. Under this examination, what counts as Universal reason, determining the direction and meaning of modernity, is revealed as the minutely determined branch or sub-species of a cultic tradition, descended from 'ranters', 'levelers', and closely related variants of dissident, ultra-protestant fanaticism, and owing vanishingly little to the conclusions of logicians.

Ironically, then, the world's regnant *Universalist* democratic-egalitarian faith is a particular or peculiar cult that has broken out, along identifiable historical and geographical pathways, with an epidemic virulence that is disguised as progressive global enlightenment. The route that it has taken,

Part 4: Re-Running the Race to Ruin

through England and New England, Reformation and Revolution, is recorded by an accumulation of traits that provide abundant material for irony, and for lower varieties of comedy. The unmasking of the modern 'liberal' intellectual or 'open-minded' media 'truth-teller' as a pale, fervent, narrowly doctrinaire puritan, recognizably descended from the species of witch-burning zealots, is reliably—and irresistibly—entertaining.

Yet, as the Cathedral extends and tightens its grip upon everything, everywhere, in accordance with its divine mandate, the response it triggers is only atypically humorous. More commonly, when unable to exact humble compliance, it encounters inarticulate rage, or at least uncomprehending, smoldering resentment, as befits the imposition of parochial cultural dogmas, still wrapped in the trappings of a specific, alien pedigree, even as they earnestly confess to universal rationality.

Consider, for instance, the most famous words of America's *Declaration of Independence*: 'We hold these truths to be self-evident, that all men are created equal, that they are endowed by their Creator with certain unalienable Rights [...]'[2] Could it be honestly maintained that to submit, scrupulously and sincerely, to such 'self-evident' truths amounts to anything other than an act of religious re-confirmation or conversion? Or denied that, in these words, reason and evidence are explicitly set aside, to make room for principles of faith? Could anything be less scientific than such a declaration, or more indiffer-

---

2 "Declaration of Independence: A Transcription," National Archives, accessed August 03, 2022, https://www.archives.gov/founding-docs/declaration-transcript.

ent to the criteria of genuinely universal reasoning? How could anybody who was not already a believer be expected to consent to such assumptions?

That the founding statement of the democratic-republican creed should be formulated as a statement of pure (and doctrinally recognizable) faith is information of sorts, but it is not yet irony. The irony begins with the fact that among the elites of today's Cathedral, these words of the Declaration of Independence (as well as many others) would be found—almost universally—to be quaintly suggestive at best, perhaps vaguely embarrassing, and most certainly incapable of supporting literal assent. Even amongst libertarian-slanted conservatives, a firm commitment to 'natural rights' is unlikely to proceed confidently and emphatically to their divine origination. For modern 'liberals', believers in the rights-bestowing (or entitlement) State, such archaic ideas are not only absurdly dated, but positively obstructive. For that reason, they are associated less with revered predecessors than with the retarded, fundamentalist thinking of political enemies. Sophisticates of the Cathedral core understand, as Hegel did, that God is no more than deep government apprehended by infants, and as such a waste of faith (that bureaucrats could put to better use).

Since the Cathedral has ascended to global supremacy, it no longer has need for Founding Fathers, who awkwardly recall its parochial ancestry, and impede its transnational public relations. Rather, it seeks perpetual re-invigoration through their denigration. The phenomenon of the 'New Atheism', with its transparent progressive affiliations, attests abundantly to this. Paleo-puritanism must be derided in order for neo-puritanism to flourish—the meme is dead, long live the meme!

At the limit of self-parody, neo-puritan parricide takes the form of the ludicrous 'War on Christmas', in which the allies of the Cathedral sanctify the (radically unthreatened) separation of Church and State through nuisance agitation against public expressions of traditional Christian piety, and their 'Red State' dupes respond with dyspeptic outrage on cable TV shows. Like every other war against fuzzy nouns (whether 'poverty', 'drugs', or 'terror'), the outcome is predictably perverse. If resistance to the War on Christmas is not yet established as the solid center of Yuletide festivities, it can be confidently expected to become so in the future. The purposes of the Cathedral are served nonetheless, through promotion of a synthetic secularism that separates the progressive faith from its religious foundations, whilst directing attention away from the ethnically specific, dogmatic creedal content at its core.

As reactionaries go, traditional Christians are generally considered to be quite cuddly. Even the most wild-eyed fanatics of the neo-puritan orthodoxy have trouble getting genuinely excited about them (although abortion activists get close). For some real red meat, with the nerves exposed and writhing to jolts of hard stimulation, it makes far more sense to turn to another discarded and ceremonially abominated block on the progressive lineage: White Identity Politics, or (the term Moldbug opts for)[3] 'white

3 Mencius Moldbug, "Why I am Not a White Nationalist," Unqualified Reservations, November 22, 2007, accessed August 03, 2022, https://www.unqualified-reservations.org/2007/11/why-i-am-not-

nationalism'.

Just as the ratchet progress of neo-puritan social democracy is radically facilitated by the orchestrated pillorying of its embryonic religious forms, so is its trend to consistently neo-fascist political economy smoothed by the concerted repudiation of a 'neo-nazi' (or paleo-fascist) threat. It is extremely convenient, when constructing ever more nakedly corporatist or 'third position' structures of state-directed pseudo-capitalism, to be able to divert attention to angry expressions of white racial paranoia, especially when these are ornamented by clumsily modified nazi insignia, horned helmets, Leni Riefenstahl aesthetics, and slogans borrowed freely from *Mein Kampf*. In the United States (and thus, with shrinking time-lag, internationally) the icons of the Ku Klux Klan, from white bed-sheets, quasi-Masonic titles, and burning crosses, to lynching ropes, have acquired comparable theatrical value.

Moldbug offers a sanitized white nationalist blog reading list, consisting of writers who—to varying degrees of success—avoid immediate reversion to paleo-fascist self-parody. The first step beyond the boundary of respectable opinion is represented by Lawrence Auster,[4] a Christian, anti-Darwinist, and 'Traditionalist Conservative' who defends 'substantial' (ethno-racial) national identity and opposes the liberal master-principle of nondiscrimination. By the time we reach 'Tanstaafl',[5] at the ripped outer

white-nationalist/.
4 View from the Right, accessed August 03, 2022, http://www.amnation.com/vfr/.
5 Age of Treason, accessed August 10, 2022, http://age-of-treason.com/

edge of Moldbug's carefully truncated spectrum, we have entered a decaying orbit, spiraling into the great black hole that is hidden at the dead center of modern political possibility.

Before following the Tanstaafl-types into the crushing abyss where light dies, there are some preliminary remarks to make about the white nationalist perspective, and its implications. Even more than the Christian traditionalists (who, even in their cultural mid-winter, can bask in the warmth of supernatural endorsement), white identity politics considers itself *besieged*. Moderate or measured concern offers no equilibrium for those who cross the line, and begin to self-identify in these terms. Instead, the path of involvement demands rapid acceleration to a state of extreme alarm, or racial panic, conforming to an analysis focused upon malicious population replacement at the hands of a government which, in the oft-cited words of Bertolt Brecht, "has decided to dissolve the people, and to appoint another one." 'Whiteness' (whether conceived biologically, mystically, or both) is associated with vulnerability, fragility, and persecution. This theme is so basic, and so multifarious, that it is difficult to adequately address succinctly. It encompasses everything from criminal predation (especially racially-charged murders, rapes, and beatings), economic exactions and inverse discrimination, cultural aggression by hostile academic and media systems, and ultimately 'genocide'—or definitive racial destruction.

Typically, the prospective annihilation of the white race is attributed to its own systematic vulnerability, whether due to characteristic cultural traits (excessive altruism, susceptibility to moral manipulation, excessive hospitality, trust, universal reciprocity, guilt, or individualistic disdain for group identity), or more immediate biological factors (recessive genes supporting fragile Aryan phenotypes). Whilst it is unlikely that this sense of unique endangerment is reducible to the chromatic formula 'White + Color = Color', the fundamental structure is of this kind. In its abstract depiction of non-reciprocal vulnerability, it reflects the 'one drop rule' (and Mendelian recessive/dominant gene combination). It depicts mixture as essentially anti-white.

Because 'whiteness' is a limit (pure absence of color), it slips smoothly from the biological factuality of the Caucasian sub-species into metaphysical and mystical ideas. Rather than accumulating genetic variation, a white race is contaminated or polluted by admixtures that compromise its defining negativity—to darken it is to destroy it. The mythological density of these—predominantly subliminal—associations invests white identity politics with a resilience that frustrates enlightened efforts at rationalistic denunciation, whilst contradicting its own paranoid self-representation. It also undermines recent white nationalist promotions of a racial threat that is strictly comparable to that facing indigenous peoples, universally, and depicting whites as 'natives' cruelly deprived of equal protection against extinction. There is no route back to tribal innocence, or flat, biological diversity. Whiteness has been compacted indissolubly with ideology, whichever the road taken.

"If Blacks can have it, and Hispanics can have it, and Jews can have it, why can't we have it?"—That's the final building block of white nationalist grievance, the werewolf curse that means it can only ever be a monster. There's exactly one way out for persecuted palefaces, and it leads straight into a black hole. We promised to get back to Tanstaafl, and here[6] we are, in late Summer 2007, shortly after he got 'the Jew thing'.[7] There isn't anything very original about his epiphany, which is exactly the point. He quotes himself:

> Isn't it absurd that anyone would even think to blame Christianity or WASPs for the rise of PC and its catastrophic consequences? Isn't this in fact a reversal of the truth? Hasn't the rise and spread of PC eroded the power of Christianity, WASPs, and whites in general? Blaming them is in effect blaming the victim.
>
> Yes, there are Christians, WASPs, and whites who have fallen for the PC brainwashing. Yes, there are some who have taken it so deeply to heart that they work to expand and protect it. That's the nature of PC. That is its purpose. To control the minds of the people it seeks to destroy. The left, at its root, is all about destruction.
>
> You don't have to be an anti-Semite to notice where these ideas originate from and who benefits. But you do have to violate PC to say: Jews.

That's the labyrinth, the trap, with its pitifully constricted, stereotypical circuit. "Why can't we be cuddly racial preservationists, like Amazonian Indians?

---

6 Content no longer available.
7 Content no longer available.

How come we always turn into Neo-Nazis? It's some kind of conspiracy, which means *it has to be the Jews*." Since the mid-20th century, the political intensity of the globalized world has streamed, almost exclusively, out of the cratered ash-pile of the Third Reich. Until you get the pattern, it seems mysterious that there's no getting away from it. After listing some blogs falling under the relatively genteel category of 'white nationalism', Moldbug cautions:

> The Internet is also home to many out-and-out racist blogs. Most are simply unreadable. But some are hosted by relatively capable writers [...] On these racist blogs you'll find racial epithets, anti-Semitism (see why I am not an anti-Semite[8]) and the like. Obviously, I cannot recommend any of these blogs, and nor will I link to them. However, if you are interested in the mind of the modern racist, Google will get you there.[9]

Google is overkill. A little link-trawling will get you there. It's a 'six degrees of separation' problem (and more like two, or less). Start digging into the actually existing 'reactosphere', and things get quite astoundingly ugly very quickly. Yes, there really is 'hate',

---

[8] Mencius Moldbug, "Why I am Note an Anti-Semite," Unqualified Reservations, June 23, 2007, accessed August 03, 2022, https://www.unqualified-reservations.org/2007/06/why-i-am-not-anti-semite/.

[9] Mencius Moldbug, "Why I am Not a White Nationalist," Unqualified Reservations, November 22, 2007, accessed August 03, 2022, https://www.unqualified-reservations.org/2007/11/why-i-am-not-white-nationalist/.

panic, and disgust, as well as a morbidly addictive abundance of very grim, vitriolic wit, and a disconcertingly impressive weight of credible fact (these guys just *love* statistics to death). Most of all, just beyond the horizon, there's the black hole. If reaction ever became a popular movement, its few slender threads of bourgeois (or perhaps dreamily 'aristocratic') civility wouldn't hold back the beast for long.

As liberal decency has severed itself from intellectual integrity, and exiled harsh truths, these truths have found new allies, and become considerably harsher. The outcome is mechanically, and monotonously, predictable. Every liberal democratic 'cause war' strengthens and feralizes what it fights. The war on poverty creates a chronically dysfunctional underclass. The war on drugs creates crystallized super-drugs and mega-mafias. Guess what? The war on political incorrectness creates data-empowered, web-coordinated, paranoid and poly-conspiratorial werewolves, superbly positioned to take advantage of liberal democracy's impending rendezvous with ruinous reality, and to then play their part in the unleashing of unpleasantnesses that are scarcely imaginable (except by disturbing historical analogy). When a sane, pragmatic, and fact-based negotiation of human differences is forbidden by ideological fiat,[10] the alternative is not a reign of perpetual peace, but a festering of increasingly self-conscious and militantly defiant *thoughtcrime*, nourished by public-

---

10 Jason Malloy, "James Watson Tells the Inconvenient Truth: Faces the Consequences," October 31, 2007, accessed August 03, 2022, http://www.gnxp.com/blog/2007/10/james-watson-tells-inconvenient-truth_296.php.

ly unavowable realities, and energized by powerful, atavistic, and palpably dissident mythologies. That's obvious, on the 'Net.

Moldbug considers the danger of white nationalism to be both over- and understated. On the one hand, the 'menace' is simply ridiculous, and merely reflects neo-puritan spiritual dogma in its most hysterically oppressive and stubbornly mindless form. "It should be obvious that, although I am not a white nationalist, I am not exactly allergic to the stuff," Moldbug remarks, before describing it as "the most marginalized and socially excluded belief system in the history of the world [...] an obnoxious social irritant in any circle which does not include tattooed speedfreak bikers."

Yet the danger remains, or rather, is *under construction*.

> I can imagine one possibility which might make white nationalism genuinely dangerous. White nationalism would be dangerous if there was some issue on which white nationalists were right, and everyone else was wrong. Truth is always dangerous. Contrary to common belief, it does not always prevail. But it's always a bad idea to turn your back on it. [...] While the evidence for human cognitive biodiversity is indeed debatable, what's not debatable is that it is debatable [...] [even though] everyone who is not a white nationalist has spent the last 50 years informing us that it is not debatable [...]

There's far more to Moldbug's essay, as there always is. Eventually it explains why he rejects white nationalism, on grounds that owe nothing to conventional reflexes. But the dark heart of the essay, lifting it beyond brilliance to the brink of genius, is found early on, at the edge of a black hole:

> Why does white nationalism strike us as evil? Because Hitler was a white nationalist, and Hitler was evil. Neither of these statements is remotely controvertible. There is exactly one degree of separation between white nationalism and evil. And that degree is Hitler. Let me repeat: Hitler.
>
> The argument seems watertight. (Hitlertight?) But it holds no water at all.
>
> Why does socialism strike us as evil? Because Stalin was a socialist, and Stalin was evil. Anyone who wants to seriously argue that Stalin was less evil than Hitler has an awful long row to hoe. Not only did Stalin order more murders, his murder machine had its heyday in peacetime, whereas Hitler's can at least be seen as a war crime against enemy civilians. Whether this makes a difference can be debated, but if it does it puts Stalin on top.
>
> And yet I have never had or seen anything like the "red flags" response to socialism ["the sense of the presence of evil"]. If I saw a crowd of young, fashionable people lining up at the box office for a hagiographic biopic on Reinhard Heydrich, chills would run up and down my neck. For Ernesto Guevara, I have no emotional response. Perhaps I think it's stupid and sad. I do think it's stupid and sad. But it doesn't freak me out.

Any attempt to be nuanced, balanced, or proportional in the moral case against Hitler is to entirely misconstrue the nature of the phenomenon. This can be noted, quite regularly, in Asian societies, for instance, because the ghost of the Third Reich does not occupy central position in their history, or rather, their *religion*, although—as the inner sanctum of the Cathedral—it is determined to (and shows almost every sign of succeeding). A brief digression on cross-cultural misunderstanding and reciprocal blindness might be merited at this point. When Westerners pay attention to the 'God-Emperor' style of political devotion that has accompanied modern totalitarianism in East Asia, the conclusion typically drawn is that this pattern of political feeling is exotically alien, morbidly amusing, and ultimately—chillingly—incomprehensible. Contemporary comparisons with laughably non-numinous Western democratic leaders only deepen the confusion, as do clumsy quasi-Marxist references to 'feudal' sensibilities (as if absolute monarchy was not an alternative to feudalism, and as if absolute monarchs were worshipped). *How could a historical and political figure ever be invested with the transcendent dignity of absolute religious meaning?* It seems absurd…

"Look, I'm not saying that Hitler was a particularly nice guy…"—to imagine such words is already to see many things. It might even provoke the question: Does anybody within the (Cathedral's) globalized world still think that Adolf Hitler was less evil than the Prince of Darkness himself? Perhaps only a few scattered paleo-Christians (who stubbornly insist that Satan is really, *really* bad), and an even smaller number of Neo-Nazi ultras (who think Hitler was kind of cool). For pretty much everybody else, Hitler *perfectly* personifies demonic monstrosity, transcending history and politics to attain the stature of a metaphysical absolute: evil incarnate. Beyond Hitler it is impossible to go, or think. This is surely interesting, since it indicates an irruption of the infinite within history—a religious revelation, of inverted, yet structurally familiar, Abrahamic type. ('Holocaust Theology' already implies as much.)

In this regard, rather than Satan, it might be more helpful to compare Hitler to the Antichrist, which is to say: to a mirror Messiah, of reversed moral polarity. There was even an empty tomb. *Hitlerism*, neutrally conceived, therefore, is less a pro-Nazi ideology than a universal faith, speciated within the Abrahamic super-family, and united in acknowledging the coming of pure evil on earth. Whilst not exactly worshipped (outside the extraordinarily disreputable circles already ventured into), Hitler is sacramentally abhorred, in a way that touches upon theological 'first things'. If to embrace Hitler as God is a sign of highly lamentable politico-spiritual confusion (at best), to recognize his historical singularity and sacred meaning is near-mandatory, since he is affirmed by all men of sound faith as the exact complement of the incarnate God (the revealed anti-Messiah, or Adversary), and this identification has the force of 'self-evident truth'. (Did anybody ever need to ask why the *reductio ad Hitlerum* works?)

Conveniently, like the secularized neo-puritanism that it swallows, (aversive) Hitlerism can be safely taught in American schools, at a remarkably high level of religious intensity. Insofar as progressive or programmatic history continues, this suggests that the Church of Sacred Hitlerite Abomination will eventually supplant its Abrahamic predecessors, to become the world's triumphant ecumenical faith. How could it not? After all, unlike vanilla deism, this is a faith that fully reconciles religious enthusiasm with enlightened opinion, equally adapted, with consummate amphibious capability, to the convulsive ecstasies of popular ritual and the letter pages of the *New York Times*. "Absolute evil once walked amongst us, and lives still..." How is this not, already, the principal religious message of our time? All that remains unfinished is the mythological consolidation, and that has long been underway.

There's still some bone-fragment picking to do among the ashes and debris [in Part 5], before turning to healthier things...

Part 4a: A Multi-Part Sub-Digression into Racial Terror

My own sense of the thing is that underneath the happy talk, underneath the dogged adherence to failed ideas and dead theories, underneath the shrieking and anathematizing at people like me, there is a deep and cold despair. In our innermost hearts, we don't believe racial harmony can be attained. Hence the trend to separation. We just want to get on with our lives away from each other. Yet for a moralistic, optimistic people like Americans, this despair is unbearable. It's pushed away somewhere we don't have to think about it. When someone forces us to think about it, we react with fury. That little boy in the Andersen story about the Emperor's new clothes? The ending would be more true to life if he had been lynched by a howling mob of outraged citizens.

— John Derbyshire, interviewed at Gawker

We believe in the equal dignity and presumption of equal decency toward every person—no matter what race, no matter what science tells us about comparative intelligence, and no mat-

ter what is to be gleaned from crime statistics. It is important that research be done, that conclusions not be rigged, and that we are at liberty to speak frankly about what it tells us. But that is not an argument for a priori conclusions about how individual persons ought to be treated in various situations—or for calculating fear or friendship based on race alone. To hold or teach otherwise is to prescribe the disintegration of a pluralistic society, to undermine the aspiration of E Pluribus Unum.

— Andrew McCarthy, defending the expulsion of JD from the National Review

"The Talk" as black Americans and liberals present it (to wit: necessitated by white malice), is a comic affront—because no one is allowed (see Barro above) to notice the context in which black Americans are having run-ins with the law, each other, and others. The proper context for understanding this, and the mania that is the Trayvonicus for that matter, is the reasonable fear of violence. This is the single most exigent fact here—yet you decree it must not be spoken.

— Dennis Dale, responding to Josh Barro's call for JD's 'firing'

Quite an experience to live in fear, isn't it? That's what it is to be a slave.

— Bladerunner

THERE is no part of Singapore, Hong Kong, Taipei, Shanghai, or very many other East Asian cities where it is impossible to wander, safely, late at night. Women, whether young or old, on their own

Part 4a: A Sub-Digression into Racial Terror

or with small children, can be comfortably oblivious to the details of space and time, at least insofar as the threat of assault is concerned. Whilst this might not be quite sufficient to define a civilized society, it comes extremely close. It is certainly *necessary* to any such definition. The contrary case is barbarism.

These lucky cities of the western Pacific Rim are typified by geographical locations and demographic profiles that conspicuously echo the embarrassingly well-behaved 'model minorities' of Occidental countries. They are (non-obnoxiously) dominated by populations that—due to biological heredity, deep cultural traditions, or some inextricable entanglement of the two—find polite, prudent, and pacific social interactions comparatively effortless, and worthy of continuous reinforcement. They are also, importantly, open, cosmopolitan societies, remarkably devoid of chauvinistic boorishness or paranoid ethno-nationalist sentiment. Their citizens are disinclined to emphasize their own virtues. On the contrary, they will typically be modest about their individual and collective attributes and achievements, abnormally sensitive to their failures and shortcomings, and constantly alert to opportunities for improvement. Complacency is almost as rare as delinquency. In these cities an entire—and massively consequential—dimension of social terror is simply absent.

In much of the Western world, in stark contrast, barbarism has been normalized. It is considered simply obvious that cities have 'bad areas' that are not merely impoverished, but lethally menacing to outsiders and residents alike. Visitors are warned to stay away, whilst locals do their best to transform their homes into fortresses, avoid venturing onto the streets after dark, and—especially if young and male—turn to criminal gangs for protection, which further degrades the security of everybody else. Predators control public space, parks are death traps, aggressive menace is celebrated as 'attitude', property acquisition is for mugs (or muggers), educational aspiration is ridiculed, and non-criminal business activity is despised as a violation of cultural norms. Every significant mechanism of socio-cultural pressure, from interpreted heritage and peer influences to political rhetoric and economic incentives, is aligned to the deepening of complacent depravity and the ruthless extirpation of every impulse to self-improvement. Quite clearly, these are places where civilization has fundamentally collapsed, and a society that includes them has to some substantial extent *failed*.

Within the most influential countries of the English-speaking world, the disintegration of urban civilization has profoundly shaped the structure and development of cities. In many cases, the 'natural' (one might now say 'Asian') pattern, in which intensive urbanization and corresponding real estate values are greatest in the downtown core, has been shattered, or at least deeply deformed. Social disintegration of the urban center has driven an exodus of the (even moderately) prosperous to suburban and exurban refuges, producing a grotesque and historically unprecedented pattern of 'donut'-style development, with cities tolerating—or merely accommodating themselves to—ruined and rotting interiors, where sane people fear to tread. 'Inner city' has come to mean almost exactly the opposite of what an undistorted course of urban development

Part 4a: A Sub-Digression into Racial Terror

would produce. This is the geographical expression of a Western—and especially American—social problem that is at once basically unmentionable and visible from outer space.

Surprisingly, the core-crashed donut syndrome has a notably insensitive yet commonly accepted name, which captures it in broad outlines—at least according to its secondary characteristics—and to a reasonable degree of statistical approximation: *White Flight*. This is an arresting term, for a variety of reasons. It is stamped, first of all, by the racial bi-polarity that—as a *vital archaism*—resonates with America's chronic social crisis at a number of levels. Whilst superficially outdated in an age of many-hued multicultural and immigration issues, it reverts to the undead code inherited from slavery and segregation, perpetually identified with Faulkner's words: "The past is not dead. It isn't even past." Yet even in this untypical moment of racial candor, blackness is elided, and implicitly disconnected from agency. It is denoted only by allusion, as a residue, concentrated passively and derivatively by the sifting function of a highly-adrenalized white panic. What *cannot be said* is indicated even as it is unmentioned. A distinctive silence accompanies the broken, half-expression of a mute tide of racial separatism, driven by civilizationally disabling terrors and animosities, whose depths, and structures of reciprocity, remain unavowable.

What the puritan exodus from Old to New World was to the foundation of Anglophone global modernity, white flight is to its fraying and dissolution. As with the pre-founding migration, what gives white flight ineluctable relevance here is its sub-political character: *all exit and no voice*. It is the subtle, non-argumentative, non-demanding 'other' of social democracy and its dreams—the spontaneous impulse of dark enlightenment, as it is initially glimpsed, at once disillusioning and implacable.

The core-crashed donut is not the only model of sick city syndrome (the shanty fringe phenomenon emphasized in Mike Davis' *Planet of Slums* is very different).[1] Nor is donut-disaster urbanism reducible to racial crisis, at least in its origins. Technological factors have played a crucial role (most prominently, automobile geography) as have quite other, long-standing cultural traditions (such as the construction of suburbia as a bourgeois idyll). Yet all such lineages have been in very large measure supplanted by, or at least subordinated to, the inherited, and still emerging, 'race problem.'

So what is this 'problem'? How is it developing? Why should anybody outside America be concerned about it? Why raise the topic now (if ever)?—If your heart is sinking under the gloomy suspicion this is going to be huge, meandering, nerve-wracking, and torturous, you're right. We've got weeks in this chamber of horrors to look forward to.

The two simplest, quite widely held, and basically incompatible answers to the first question deserve to be considered as important parts of the problem.

> Question: What is America's race problem?
>
> Answer 1: Black people.
> Answer 2: White people.

The combined popularity of these options is significantly expanded, most probably to encompass

---

[1] Mike Davis, *Planet of Slums* (London: Verso, 2006).

Part 4a: A Sub-Digression into Racial Terror

a large majority of all Americans, when it is taken to include those who assume that one of these two answers dominates the thinking of the *other side*. Between them, the propositions "the problem would be over if we could just rid ourselves of black hoodlums/white racists" and/or "they think we're all hoodlums/racists and want to get rid of us" consume an impressive proportion of the political spectrum, establishing a solid foundation of reciprocal terror and aversion. When defensive projections are added ("we're not hoodlums, you're racists" or "we're not racists, you're hoodlums"), the potential for super-heated, non-synthesizing dialectics approaches the infinite.

Not that these 'sides' are racial (except in black or white tribal-nationalist fantasy).[2] For crude stereotypes, it is far more useful to turn to the principal political dimension, and its categories of 'liberal' and 'conservative' in the contemporary, American sense. To identify America's race problem with white racism is the stereotypical *liberal* position, whilst identifying it with black social dysfunction is the exact *conservative* complement. Although these stances are formally symmetrical, it is their actual political *asymmetry* that charges the American race problem with its extraordinary historical dynamism and universal significance.

That American whites and blacks—considered crudely as statistical aggregates—co-exist in a rela-

---

2 Mencius Moldbug, "Why I am Not a White Nationalist," Unqualified Reservations, November 22, 2007, accessed August 03, 2022, https://www.unqualified-reservations.org/2007/11/why-i-am-not-white-nationalist/.

tion of reciprocal fear and perceived victimization, is attested by the manifest patterns of urban development and navigation, school choice, gun ownership, policing and incarceration, and just about every other expression of *revealed* (as opposed to *stated*) preference that is related to voluntary social distribution and security. An objective balance of terror reigns, erased from visibility by complementary yet incompatible perspectives of victimological supremacism and denial. Yet between *the liberal and conservative positions on race* there is no balance whatsoever, but something closer to a rout. Conservatives are utterly terrified of the issue, whilst for liberals it is a garden of earthly delight, whose pleasures transcend the limits of human understanding. When any political discussion firmly and clearly arrives at the topic of race, liberalism wins. That is the fundamental law of ideological effectiveness in the fragrant shade of the Cathedral. In certain respects, this dynamic political imbalance is even the primary phenomenon under consideration (and much more needs to be said about it, down the road).

The regular, excruciating, soul-crushing humiliation of conservatism on the race issue should come as no surprise to anybody. After all, the principal role of conservatism in modern politics is to be humiliated. That is what a perpetual loyal opposition, or court jester, is for. The essential character of liberalism, as guardian and proponent of neo-puritan spiritual truth, invests it with supreme mastery over the dialectic, or invulnerability to contradiction. *That which it is impossible to think must necessarily be embraced through faith.* Consider only the fundamental doctrine or first article of the liberal creed, as pro-

Part 4a: A Sub-Digression into Racial Terror

mulgated through every public discussion, academic articulation, and legislative initiative relevant to the topic: *Race doesn't exist, except as a social construct employed by one race to exploit and oppress another.* Merely to entertain it is to shudder before the awesome majesty of the absolute, where everything is simultaneously its precise opposite, and reason evaporates ecstatically at the brink of the sublime.

If the world was built out of ideology, this story would already be over, or at least predictably programmed. Beyond the apparent zig-zag of the dialectic there is a dominant trend, heading in a single, unambiguous direction. Yet the liberal-progressive solution to the race problem—open-endedly escalating, comprehensively systematic, dynamically paradoxical 'anti-racism'—confronts a real obstacle that is only very partially reflected in conservative attitudes, rhetoric, and ideology. The real enemy, glacial, inchoate, and non-argumentative, is 'white flight'.

At this point, explicit reference to the Derbyshire Case becomes irresistible. There is a very considerable amount of complex, recent historical context that cries out for introduction—the cultural convulsion attending the Trayvon Martin incident in particular—but there'll be time for that later (oh yes, I'm afraid so). Derbyshire's intervention, and the explosion of words it provoked, while to some extent illuminated by such context, far exceeds it. That is because the crucial unspoken term, both in Derbyshire's now-notorious short article, and also—apparently—in the responses it generated, is 'white flight'.[3] By publishing paternal advice to his (Eurasian) children that has been—not entirely unreasonably—summarized as 'avoid black people', he converted white flight from a much-lamented but seemingly inexorable fact into an explicit imperative, even a *cause*. *Don't argue, flee.*

The word Derbyshire emphasizes, in his own penumbra of commentary, and in antecedent writings, is not 'flight' or 'panic', but *despair*. When asked by blogger Vox Day whether he agreed that the 'race card' had become less intimidating over the past two decades, Derbyshire replies:

> One [factor], which I've written about more than once, I think, in the United States, is just despair. I am of a certain age, and I was around 50 years ago. I was reading the newspapers and following world events and I remember the civil rights movement. I was in England, but we followed it. I remember it, I remember what we felt about it, and what people were writing about it. It was full of hope. The idea in everyone's mind was that if we strike down these unjust laws and we outlaw all this discrimination, then we'll be whole. Then America will be made whole. After an intermediate period of a few years, who knows, maybe 20 years, with a hand up from things like affirmative action, black America will just merge into the general population and the whole thing will just go

---

3   John Derbyshire, "The Talk: Nonblack Version," Taki's Magazine, April 05, 2012, accessed August 04, 2022, https://www.takimag.com/article/the_talk_nonblack_version_john_derbyshire/.

Part 4a: A Sub-Digression into Racial Terror

> away. That's what everybody believed. Everybody thought that. And it didn't happen.
>
> Here we are, we're 50 years later, and we've still got these tremendous disparities in crime rates, educational attainment, and so on. And I think, although they're still mouthing the platitudes, Americans in their hearts feel a kind of cold despair about it. They feel that Thomas Jefferson was probably right and we can't live together in harmony. I think that's why you see this slow ethnic disaggregation. We have a very segregated school system now. There are schools within 10 miles of where I'm sitting that are 98 percent minority. In residential housing too, it's the same thing. So I think there is a cold, dark despair lurking in America's collective heart about the whole thing.[4]

This is a version of reality that few want to hear. As Derbyshire recognizes, Americans are a predominantly Christian, optimistic, 'can-do' people, whose 'collective heart' is unusually maladapted to an *abandonment of hope*. This is a country culturally hardwired to interpret despair not merely as error or weakness, but as *sin*. Nobody who understands this could be remotely surprised to find bleak hereditarian fatalism being rejected—typically with vehement hostility—not only by progressives, but also by the overwhelming majority of conservatives. At NRO, Andrew C. McCarthy no doubt spoke for many in remarking:

> There is a world of difference, though, be-

---

4 Content no longer available.

tween the need to be able to discuss uncomfortable facts about IQ and incarceration, on the one hand, and, on the other, to urge race as a rationale for abandoning basic Christian charity.

Others went much further. At the Examiner, James Gibson seized upon "John Derbyshire's vile racist screed" as the opportunity to teach a wider lesson—"the danger of conservatism divorced from Christianity":

> [...] since Derbyshire does not believe "that Jesus of Nazareth was divine [...] and that the Resurrection was a real event," he cannot comprehend the great mystery of the Incarnation, whereby the Divine truly did take on human flesh in the person of Jesus of Nazareth and suffered death at the hands of a fallen humanity in order to redeem that humanity out of its state of fallenness.
>
> Herein lies the danger of a conservative socio-political philosophy divorced from a robust Christian faith. It becomes a dead ideology spawning a view of humanity that is toxic, fatalistic, and (as Derbyshire proves abundantly) uncharitable.[5]

It was, of course, on the left that the fireworks truly ignited. Elspeth Reeve at the Atlantic Wire contended that Derbyshire had clung on to his relation with the National Review because he was offering the magazine's "less enlightened readers" what they

---

5 Content no longer available.

Part 4a: A Sub-Digression into Racial Terror

wanted: "dated racial stereotypes."[6] Like Gibson on the right, she was keen for people to learn a wider lesson: don't think for a minute this stops with Derbyshire. (The stunningly uncooperative comments thread to her article is worth noting.)

At Gawker, Louis Peitzman jumped the shark (in the approved direction) by describing Derbyshire's "horrifying diatribe" as the "most racist article possible," a judgment that betrays extreme historical ignorance, a sheltered life, unusual innocence, and a lack of imagination, as well as making the piece sound far more interesting than it actually is.[7] Peitzman's commentators are impeccably liberal, and of course uniformly, utterly, shatteringly appalled (to the point of orgasm). Beyond the emoting, Peitzman doesn't offer much content, excepting only a little extra emoting—this time mild satisfaction mixed with residual rage—at the news that Derbyshire's punishment has at least begun ("a step in the right direction") with his "canning" from the *National Review*.

Joanna Schroeder (writing at something called the Good Feed Blog) sought to extend the purge beyond Derbyshire, to include anybody who had not yet

---

6 Elspeth Reeve, "Why John Derbyshire hasn't been Fired (Yet)," The Wire, April 06, 2012, accessed August 04, 2022, https://web.archive.org/web/20161126070030/http://www.thewire.com/politics/2012/04/why-john-derbyshire-hasnt-been-fired-yet/50803//.

7 Louis Peitzman, "Racist John Derbyshire Fired for Writing most Racist Article Possible," Gawker, August 04, 2012, accessed August 04, 2022, https://www.gawker.com/5900109/racist-john-derbyshire-fired-for-writing-most-racist-article-possible.

erupted into sufficiently melodramatic paroxysms of indignation, starting with David Weigel at Slate[8] (who she doesn't know "in real life, but in reading this piece, it seems you just might be a racist, pal"). "There are so many [...] racist, dehumanizing references to black people in Derbyshire's article that I have to just stop myself here before I recount the entire thing point by point with fuming rage," she shares. Unlike Peitzman, however, at least Schroeder has a point—the racial terror dialectic—"[...] propagating the idea that we should be afraid of black men, of black people in general, makes this world dangerous for innocent Americans."[9] *Your fear makes you scary* (although apparently not with legitimate reciprocity).

As for Weigel, he gets the terror good and hard. Within hours he's back at the keyboard, apologizing for his previous insouciance, and for the fact he "never ended up saying the obvious: People, the essay was disgusting."[10]

So what did Derbyshire actually say, where did it come from, and what does it mean to American politics (and beyond)? This sub-series will comb

---

8 Davis Weigel, "John Derbyshire's Advice for White People," Slate, April 06, 2012, accessed August 04, 2022, https://slate.com/news-and-politics/2012/04/john-derbyshire-s-advice-for-white-people.html.
9 Joanna Schroeder, "Racist Writings: Should Derbyshire and Weigel be Fired?", April 07, 2012, accessed August 04, 2022, https://goodmenproject.com/good-feed-blog/racist-writings-should-derbyshire-and-weigel-be-fired/.
10 David Weigel, "Derbyshire Again," Slate, April 07, 2012, accessed August 04, 2022, https://slate.com/news-and-politics/2012/04/derbyshire-again.html.

Part 4a: A Sub-Digression into Racial Terror

through the spectrum from left to right in search of suggestions, with socio-geographically manifested 'white' panic/despair as a guiding thread [...]

Coming next: The Liberal Ecstasy

Part 4b: Obnoxious Observations

Although black families and parents of boys aren't the only ones who worry about the safety of adolescents, Tillman, Brown and other parents say raising black boys is perhaps the most stressful aspect of parenting because they're dealing with a society that is fearful and hostile toward them, simply because of the color of their skin.

"Don't believe it? Walk a day in my shoes," Brown said.

Brown said that at 14, his son is at that critical age when he's always worried about his safety because of profiling.

"I don't want to scare him or have him paint people with a broad brush, but, historically, we black males have been stigmatized as the purveyors of crime and wherever we are, we're suspect," Brown said.

Black parents who don't make that fact clear, he and others said, do it at their sons' peril.

"Any African-American parent not having that conversation is being irresponsible," Brown said. "I see this whole thing as an opportunity for us to speak frankly, openly and honestly about race relations."

— Gracie Bonds Staples (Star-Telegram)

Part 4b: Obnoxious Observations

> *When communities resist an influx of Section 8 housing-voucher holders from the inner city, say, they are reacting overwhelmingly to behavior. Skin color is a proxy for that behavior. If inner-city blacks behaved like Asians—cramming as much knowledge into their kids as they can possibly fit into their skulls—the lingering wariness towards lower-income blacks that many Americans unquestionably harbor would disappear. Are there irredeemable racists among Americans? To be sure. They come in all colors, and we should deplore all of them. But the issue of race in the United States is more complex than polite company is usually allowed to express.*
>
> — Heather MacDonald (City Journal)

> *"Let's talk about the elephant in the room. I'm black, OK?" the woman said, declining to be identified because she anticipated backlash due to her race. She leaned in to look a reporter directly in the eyes. "There were black boys robbing houses in this neighborhood," she said. "That's why George was suspicious of Trayvon Martin."*
>
> — Chris Francescani (Reuters)

"In brief, dialectics can be defined as the doctrine of the unity of opposites. This embodies the essence of dialectics," Lenin notes, "but it requires explanations and development."[1] That is to say: further discussion.

---

1 Vladimir Ilyich Lenin, "Summary of Dialectics," Marxists.org, accessed August 04, 2022, https://www.marxists.org/archive/lenin/works/1914/cons-logic/summary.htm.

The sublimation (*Aufhebung*) of Marxism into Leninism is an eventuality that is best grasped crudely. By forging a revolutionary communist politics of broad application, almost entirely divorced from the mature material conditions or advanced social contradictions that had been previously anticipated, Lenin demonstrated that dialectical tension coincided, exhaustively, with its politicization (and that all reference to a 'dialectics of nature' is no more than retrospective subordination of the scientific domain to a political model). Dialectics are as real as they are made to be.

The dialectic begins with political agitation, and extends no further than its practical, antagonistic, factional and coalitional 'logic'. It is the 'superstructure' *for itself*, or against natural limitation, practically appropriating the political sphere in its broadest graspable extension as a platform for social domination. Everywhere that there is argument, there is an unresolved opportunity to rule.

The Cathedral incarnates these lessons. It has no need to espouse Leninism, or operational communist dialectics, because it recognizes nothing else. There is scarcely a fragment of the social 'superstructure' that has escaped dialectical reconstruction, through articulate antagonism, polarization, binary structuring, and reversal. Within the academy, the media, even the fine arts, political super-saturation has prevailed, identifying even the most minuscule elements of apprehension with conflictual 'social critique' and egalitarian teleology. Communism is the universal implication.

More dialectics is more politics, and more politics means 'progress'—or social migration to the

Part 4b: Obnoxious Observations

left. The production of public agreement only leads in one direction, and within public disagreement, such impetus already exists in embryo. It is only in the absence of agreement *and* of publicly articulated disagreement, which is to say, in non-dialectics, non-argument, sub-political diversity, or politically uncoordinated initiative, that the 'right-wing' refuge of 'the economy' (and civil society more widely) is to be found.

When no agreement is necessary, or coercively demanded, negative (or 'libertarian') liberty is still possible, and this non-argumentative 'other' of dialectics is easily formulated (even if, in a free society, it doesn't need to be): *Do your own thing.* Quite clearly, this irresponsible and negligent imperative is *politically* intolerable. It coincides exactly with leftist depression, retrogression, or depoliticization. Nothing cries out more urgently to be *argued against*.

At the opposite extreme lies the dialectical ecstasy of theatrical justice, in which the argumentative structure of legal proceedings is coupled with publicization through the media. Dialectical enthusiasm finds its definitive expression in a courtroom drama that combines lawyers, journalists, community activists, and other agents of the revolutionary superstructure in the production of a show trial. Social contradictions are staged, antagonistic cases articulated, and resolution institutionally expected. This is Hegel for prime-time television (and now for the Internet). It is the way that the Cathedral shares its message with the people.

Sometimes, in its impatient passion for progress, this message can trip over itself, because even though the agents of the Cathedral are *infinitely* reasonable, they are ever less sensible, often strikingly incompetent, and prone to making mistakes. This is to be expected on theological grounds. As the state becomes God, it degenerates into imbecility, on the model of the holy fool. The media-politics of the Trayvon Martin spectacle provides a pertinent example.

In the United States, as in any other large country, lots of things happen every day, exhibiting innumerable patterns of varying obscurity. For instance, on an average day, there are roughly 3,400 violent crimes, including 40 murders, 230 rapes, 1,000 robberies, and 2,100 aggravated assaults, alongside 25,000 non-violent property crimes (burglaries and thefts).[2] Very few of these will be widely publicized, or seized upon as educational, exemplary, and representative. Even were the media not inclined towards a narrative-based selection of 'good stories', the sheer volume of incidents would compel something of the kind. Given this situation, it is all but inevitable that people will ask: *Why are they telling us this?*

Almost everything about the death of Trayvon Martin is controversial, except for media motivation. On that topic there is near unanimity. The meaning or intended message of the story of the case could scarcely have been more transparent: *White racist paranoia makes America dangerous for black people.* It would thus rehearse the dialectic of racial terror (*your fear is scary*), designed—as always—to convert America's reciprocal social nightmare into a unilateral morality play, allocating legitimate dread exclusively to one side of the country's principal racial

[2] United States Crime Rates 1960–2019, disastercenter.com, accessed August 04, 2022, https://www.disastercenter.com/crime/uscrime.htm.

divide. It seemed perfect. A malignantly deluded white vigilante guns down an innocent black child, justifying black fear ('the talk') whilst exposing white panic as a murderous psychosis. This is a story of such archetypal progressive meaning that it cannot be told too many times. In fact, it was just too good to be true.

It soon became evident, however, that media selection—even when reinforced by the celebrity/'community activist' rage-machine—hadn't sufficed to keep the story on script, and both of the main actors were drifting from their assigned roles. If progressively-endorsed stereotypes were to be even remotely preserved, vigorous editing would be required.[3] This was especially necessary because certain evil, racist, bigoted readers of the Miami Herald were beginning to forge a narrative-wrecking mental connection between 'Trayvon Martin' and 'burglary tool'.[4]

As for the killer, George Zimmerman, the name said it all. He was clearly going to be a hulking, pasty-faced, storm-trooper look-alike, hopefully some kind of Christian gun-nut, and maybe—if they really hit pay-dirt—a militia movement type with a history of homophobia and anti-abortion activism. He started off 'white'—for no obvious reason beyond media incompetence and narrative programming—then

---

3 Trayvon Martin FAQ. Site has been made private. Archived at https://archive.ph/LOsTE.
4 Frances Robles, "Multiple Suspensions Paint Complicated Portrait of Trayvon Martin," Miami Herald, March 26, 2012, accessed August 04, 2022, https://web.archive.org/web/20140723091453/http://www.miamiherald.com/2012/03/26/v-fullstory/2714778/thousands-expected-at-trayvon.html.

found himself transformed into a 'white Hispanic' (a category that seems to have been rapidly innovated on the spot), before gradually shifted through a series of ever more reality-compliant ethnic complications, culminating in the discovery of his Afro-Peruvian great grandfather.

In the heart of the Cathedral it was well into head-scratching time. Here was the great Amerikkkan defendant being prepped for his show trial, the President had pitched in emotionally on behalf of the sacred victim, and the coordinated ground game had been advanced to the simmering brink of race riots, when the message began falling apart, to such an extent that it now threatened to decay into an annoyingly irrelevant case of black-on-black violence. It was not only that George Zimmerman had black ancestry—making him simply 'black' by the left's own social constructivist standards—he had also grown up amicably among black people, with two African-American girls as "part of the household for years," had entered into joint business venture with a black partner, he was a registered Democrat, and even some kind of 'community organizer'.

So why did Martin die? Was it for carrying iced tea and a bag of Skittles while black (the media and community activist approved, 'son Obama might have had' version), for scoping out burglary targets (the Kluxer racial profiling version), or for breaking Zimmerman's nose, knocking him over, sitting on top of him, and smashing his head repeatedly against the sidewalk (to be decided in court)? Was he a martyr to racial injustice, a low-level social predator, or a human symptom of American urban crisis? The only thing that was really clear when legal proceedings began, beyond the squalid sadness of the episode, was that it was not resolving anything.

For a sense of just how disconcertingly the approved lesson had disintegrated by the time Zimmerman was charged with second degree murder, it is only necessary to read this post by HBD-blogger oneSTDV, describing the dialectical derangements of the race-warrior right:

> Despite the disturbing nature of the "charges" against Zimmerman, many in the alt-right refuse to grant Zimmerman any sympathy or to even view this as a seminal moment in modern leftism's anarcho-tyrannical reign. According to these individuals, **the Spanish-speaking, registered Democrat mestizo got what was coming to him**—the ire of the black mob and the elite left indirectly buttressed by Zimmerman himself. Due to his voting record, multicultural background, and mentoring of minority youth, they see Zimmerman as emblematic of the left's assault on white America, a sort of ground soldier in the campaign against American whiteness. [Bolding in original.][5]

The pop PC police were ready to move on. With the great show trial collapsing into narrative disorder, it was time to refocus on the Message, facts be damned (and double damned). 'Jezebel' best exemplifies the hectoring, vaguely hysterical tone:

> You know how you can tell that black people are still oppressed? Because black people

---

5 Site has been made private.

are still oppressed. If you claim that you are not a racist person (or, at least, that you're committed to working your ass off not to be one—which is really the best that any of us can promise), then you must believe that people are fundamentally born equal. So if that's true, then in a vacuum, factors like skin color should have no effect on anyone's success. Right? And therefore, if you really believe that all people are created equal, then when you see that drastic racial inequalities exist in the real world, the only thing that you could possibly conclude is that some external force is holding certain people back. Like… racism. Right? So congratulations! You believe in racism! Unless you don't actually think that people are born equal. And if you don't believe that people are born equal, then you're a f*****g racist.[6]

Does anyone "really believe that people are born equal," in the way it is understood here? Believe, that is, not only that a formal expectation of equal treatment is a prerequisite for civilized interaction, but that any revealed deviation from substantial equality of outcome is an obvious, unambiguous indication of oppression? That's "the only thing you could *possibly* conclude"?

At the very least, Jezebel should be congratulated for expressing the progressive faith in its purest form, entirely uncontaminated by sensitivity to evi-

6 Lindy West, "A Complete Guide to 'Hipster Racism'," Jezebel, April 26, 2012, accessed August 04, 2022, https://jezebel.com/a-complete-guide-to-hipster-racism-5905291.

dence or uncertainty of any kind, casually contemptuous of any relevant research—whether existent or merely conceivable—and supremely confident about its own moral invincibility. If the facts are *morally wrong*, so much worse for the facts—that's the only position that could *possibly* be adopted, even if it's based upon a mixture of wishful thinking, deliberate ignorance, and insultingly childish lies.

To call the belief in substantial human equality a superstition is to insult superstition. It might be unwarranted to believe in leprechauns, but at least the person who holds to such a belief isn't *watching them not exist*, for every waking hour of the day. Human inequality, in contrast, and in all of its abundant multiplicity, is constantly on display, as people exhibit their variations in gender, ethnicity, physical attractiveness, size and shape, strength, health, agility, charm, humor, wit, industriousness, and sociability, among countless other features, traits, abilities, and aspects of their personality, some immediately and conspicuously, some only slowly, over time. To absorb even the slightest fraction of all this and to conclude, in the only way possible, that it is either nothing at all, or a 'social construct' and index of oppression, is sheer Gnostic delirium: a commitment beyond all evidence to the existence of a true and good world veiled by appearances. People are not equal, they do not develop equally, their goals and achievements are not equal, and nothing can make them equal. Substantial equality has no relation to reality, except as its systematic negation. Violence on a genocidal scale is required to even approximate to a practical egalitarian program, and if anything less ambitious is attempted, people get around it (some more competently than others).

To take only the most obvious example, anybody with more than one child knows that *nobody is born equal* (monozygotic twins and clones perhaps excepted). *In fact*, everybody is born different, in innumerable ways. Even when—as is normally the case—the implications of these differences for life outcomes are difficult to confidently predict, their existence is undeniable, or at least: sincerely undeniable. Of course sincerity, or even minimal cognitive coherence, is not remotely the issue here. Jezebel's position, whilst impeccable in its political correctness, is not only factually dubious, but rather laughably absurd, and actually—strictly speaking—insane. It dogmatizes a denial of reality so extreme that nobody could genuinely maintain, or even entertain it, let alone plausibly explain or defend it. It is a tenet of faith that cannot be understood, but only asserted, or submitted to, as madness made law, or authoritarian religion.

The political commandment of this religion is transparent: Accept progressive social policy as the *only possible* solution to the sin problem of inequality. This commandment is a 'categorical imperative'—no possible fact could ever undermine, complicate, or revise it. If progressive social policy actually results in an exacerbation of the problem, 'fallen' reality is to blame, since the social malady is *obviously* worse than had been originally envisaged, and only redoubled efforts in the same direction can hope to remedy it. There can be nothing to learn in matters of faith. Eventually, systematic social collapse teaches the lesson that chronic failure and incremental deterioration could not communicate. (That's macro-scale social Darwinism for dummies, and it's the way that civilizations end.)

Due to its exceptional correlation with substantial variation in social outcomes in modern societies, by far the most troublesome dimension of human biodiversity is intelligence or general problem-solving ability, quantified as IQ (measuring Spearman's 'g'). When 'statistical common sense' or profiling is applied to the proponents of Human Biodiversity, however, another significant trait is rapidly exposed: a remarkably consistent deficit of *agreeableness*. Indeed, it is widely accepted within the accursed 'community' itself that most of those stubborn and awkward enough to educate themselves on the topic of human biological variation are significantly 'socially retarded', with low verbal inhibition, low empathy, and low social integration, resulting in chronic maladaptation to group expectations.[7] The typical EQs of this group can be extracted as the approximate square-root of their IQs. Mild autism is typical, sufficient to approach their fellow beings in a spirit of detached, natural-scientific curiosity, but not so advanced as to compel total cosmic disengagement. These traits, which they themselves consider—on the basis of copious technical information—to be substantially heritable, have manifest social consequences, reducing employment opportunities, incomes, and even reproductive potential. Despite all the free therapeutic advice available in the progressive environment, this obnoxiousness shows no sign of diminishing, and might even be intensifying. As

---

7 Original link broken. Moved to https://www.discovermagazine.com/health/one-baby-alone-on-a-pca-island.

Jezebel shows so clearly, this can only *possibly* be a sign of structural oppression. Why can't obnoxious people get a break?

The history is damning. 'Sociables' have always had it in for the obnoxious, often declining to marry or do business with them, excluding them from group activities and political office, labeling them with slurs, ostracizing and avoiding them. 'Obnoxiousness' has been stigmatized and stereotyped in extremely negative terms, to such an extent that many of the obnoxious have sought out more sensitive labels, such as 'socially-challenged', or 'differently socially abled'. Not uncommonly, people have been verbally or even physically assaulted for no other reason than their radical obnoxiousness. Most tragically of all, due to their complete inability to get on with one another, the obnoxious have never been able to politically mobilize against the structural social oppression they face, or to enter into coalitions with their natural allies, such as cynics, debunkers, contrarians, and Tourette Syndrome sufferers. Obnoxiousness has yet to be liberated, although it's probable that the Internet will 'help'…

Consider John Derbyshire's essay in infamy, *The Talk: Nonblack Version*, focusing initially on its relentless obnoxiousness, and attentive to the negative correlation between sociability and objective reason.[8] As Derbyshire notes elsewhere, people are generally incapable of differentiating themselves from group identities, or properly applying statistical general-

---

8   John Derbyshire, "The Talk: Nonblack Version," Taki's Magazine, April 05, 2012, accessed August 04, 2022, https://www.takimag.com/article/the_talk_nonblack_version_john_derbyshire/.

izations about groups to individual cases, including their own. A rationally indefensible, but socially inevitable, reification of group profiles is psychologically normal—even 'human'—with the result that noisy, non-specific, statistical information is erroneously accepted as a contribution to self-understanding, even when specific information is available.

From the perspective of socially autistic, low-EQ, rational analysis, this is simply *mistaken*. If an individual has certain characteristics, the fact of belonging to a group that has similar or dissimilar average characteristics is of no relevance whatsoever. Direct and determinate information about the individual is not to any degree enriched by indirect and indeterminate (probabilistic) information about the groups to which the individual belongs. If an individual's test results are known, for instance, no additional insight is provided by statistical inferences about the test results that *might have been expected* based on group profiling. An Ashkenazi Jewish moron is no less moronic because he is an Ashkenazi Jew. Elderly Chinese nuns are unlikely to be murderers, but a murderer who happens to be an elderly Chinese nun is neither more nor less murderous than one who is not. This is all extremely obvious, to obnoxious people.

To normal people, however, it is not obvious at all. In part this is because rational intelligence is scarce and abnormal among humans, and in part because social 'intelligence' works with what everyone else is thinking, which is to say, with irrational groupish sentiment, meager information, prejudices, stereotypes, and heuristics. Since (almost) everybody else is taking short-cuts, or 'economizing' on reason, it is only rational to react defensively to generalizations that are likely to be reified or inappropriately applied—over-riding or substituting for specific perceptions. Anybody who anticipates being pre-defined through a group identity has an expanded ego-investment in that group and the way it is perceived. A generic assessment, however objectively arrived at, will immediately become personal, under (even quite remotely) normal conditions.

Obnoxious reason can stubbornly insist that *anything average cannot be about you*, but the message will not be generally received. Human social 'intelligence' is not built that way. Even supposedly sophisticated commentators blunder repeatedly into the most jarring exhibitions of basic statistical incomprehension without the slightest embarrassment, because embarrassment was designed for something else (and for almost exactly the opposite). The failure to understand stereotypes in their scientific, or probabilistic application, is a functional prerequisite of sociability, since the sole alternative to idiocy in this respect is obnoxiousness.

Derbyshire's article is noteworthy because it succeeds in being *definitively obnoxious*, and has been recognized as such, despite the spluttering incoherence of most rejoinders. Among the things that 'the talk' and 'the counter-talk' share is a theatrical structure of *pseudo-private conversation designed to be overheard*. In both cases, a message that parents are compelled to deliver to their children is staged as the vehicle for a wider social lesson, aimed at those who, through action or inaction, have created a world that is intolerably hazardous to them.

This form is intrinsically manipulative, making

even the 'original' talk a tempting target of parody. In the original, however, a tone of anguished sincerity is engineered through a deliberate performance of innocence (or ignorance). Listen son, I know this will be difficult to understand ... (*Oh why, oh why are they doing this to us?*). The counter-talk, in stark contrast, melds its micro-social drama with the clinically non-sociable discourse of "methodical inquiries in the human sciences"—treating populations as fuzzy bio-geographical units with quantifiable characteristics, rather than as legal-political subjects in communication. It derides innocence, and—by implication—the criterion of sociability itself. Agreement, agreeableness, count for nothing. The rigorously and redundantly compiled statistics say what they say, and if we cannot live with that, so much the worse for us.

Yet even to a reasonably sympathetic, or scrupulously obnoxious, reading, Derbyshire's article provides grounds for criticism. For instance, and from the beginning, it is notable that the racial reciprocal of "nonblack Americans" is 'black Americans', not "American blacks" (the term Derbyshire selects). This reversal of word order, switching nouns and adjectives, quickly settles into a pattern. Does it matter that Derbyshire requests the extension of civility to any "individual black" (rather than to 'black individuals')? It certainly makes a difference. To say that someone is 'black' is to say something about them, but to say that someone is 'a black' is to say who they are. The effect is subtly, yet distinctly, menacing, and Derbyshire is too well-trained, algebraically, to be excused from noticing it. After all, 'John Derbyshire is a white' sounds equally off, as does any analogous formulation, submerging the individual in the genus, to be retrieved as a mere instance, or example.

The more intellectually substantive aspect of this over-reach into gratuitous incivility have been examined by William Saletan[9] and Noah Millman,[10] who make very similar points, from the two sides of the liberal/conservative divide. Both writers identify a fissure or methodical incongruity in Derbyshire's article, stemming from its commitment to the micro-social application of macro-social statistical generalizations. Stereotypes, however rigorously confirmed, are *essentially* inferior to specific knowledge in any concrete social situation, because nobody ever encounters a population.

As a liberal of problematic standing,[11] Saletan has no choice but to recoil melodramatically from Derbyshire's "stomach-turning conclusions," but his reasons for doing so are not consumed by his gastro-emotional crisis. "But what exactly is a statistical truth?" he asks. "It's a probability estimate you might fall back on if you know nothing about [a particular individual]. It's an ignorant person's weak substitute for knowledge." Derbyshire, with his Aspergery attention to the absence of black Fields Medal win-

---

9 William Saletan, "John Derbyshire's Error: The Ignorance of Racial Profiling," Slate, April 10, 2012, accessed August 04, 2022, https://slate.com/news-and-politics/2012/04/john-derbyshire-trayvon-martin-and-the-ignorance-of-racial-profiling.html.
10 Original link broken. Archived at https://archive.ph/QiXYk.
11 William Saletan, "Liberal Creationism," Slate, November 18, 2007, accessed August 04, 2022, https://slate.com/technology/2007/11/liberal-creationism.html.

ners, is "[…] a math nerd who substitutes statistical intelligence for social intelligence. He recommends group calculations instead of taking the trouble to learn about the person standing in front of you."

Millman emphasizes the ironic reversal that switches (obnoxious) social scientific knowledge into imperative ignorance:

> The "race realists" like to say that they are the ones who are curious about the world, and the "politically correct" types are the ones who prefer to ignore ugly reality. But the advice Derbyshire gives to his children encourages them not to be too curious about the world around them, for fear of getting hurt. And, as a general rule, that's terrible advice for kids—and not the advice that Derbyshire has followed in his own life.

Millman's conclusion is also instructive:

> So why am I arguing with Derb at all? Well, because he's a friend. And because even lazy, socially-irresponsible talk deserves to be refuted, not merely denounced. Is Derbyshire's piece racist? Of course it's racist. His whole point is that it is both rational and morally right for his children to treat black people significantly differently from white people, and to fear them. But "racist" is a descriptive term, not a moral one. The "race realist" crowd is strongly convinced of the accuracy of Derbyshire's major premises, and they are not going to be argued out of that conviction by the assertion such conviction is "racist"—nor, honestly, should

they be. For that reason, I feel it's important to argue that Derbyshire's conclusions do not follow simply from those premises, and are, in fact, morally incorrect even if those premises are granted for the sake of argument.

[Brief intermission ...]

Part 4c: The Cracker Factory

In a sense we've come to our nation's capital to cash a check. When the architects of our republic wrote the magnificent words of the Constitution and the Declaration of Independence, they were signing a promissory note to which every American was to fall heir. This note was a promise that all men—yes, black men as well as white men—would be guaranteed the unalienable rights of life, liberty, and the pursuit of happiness.

It is obvious today that America has defaulted on this promissory note insofar as her citizens of color are concerned. Instead of honoring this sacred obligation, America has given the Negro people a bad check, a check that has come back marked "insufficient funds."

— Martin Luther King Jr.[1]

Conservatism [...] is a white people's movement, a scattering of outliers notwithstanding. Always has been, always will be. I have at-

---

[1] "Full Text of King's 'I Have a Dream' Speech," Chicago Tribune, January 31, 2013, accessed August 04, 2022, https://www.chicagotribune.com/nation-world/sns-mlk-ihaveadream-story.html.

tended at least a hundred conservative gatherings, conferences, cruises, and jamborees: let me tell you, there ain't too many raisins in that bun. I was in and out of the National Review offices for twelve years, and the only black person I saw there, other than when Herman Cain came calling, was Alex, the guy who runs the mail room. (Hey, Alex!)

This isn't because conservatism is hostile to blacks and mestizos. Very much the contrary, especially in the case of Conservatism Inc. They fawn over the occasional nonwhite with a puppyish deference that fairly fogs the air with embarrassment. (Q: What do you call the one black guy at a gathering of 1,000 Republicans? A: "Mr. Chairman.")

It's just that conservative ideals like self-sufficiency and minimal dependence on government have no appeal to underperforming minorities—groups who, in the statistical generality, are short of the attributes that make for group success in a modern commercial nation.

Of what use would it be to them to embrace such ideals? They would end up even more decisively pooled at the bottom of society than they are currently.

A much better strategy for them is to ally with as many disaffected white and Asian subgroups as they can (homosexuals, feminists, dead-end labor unions), attain electoral majorities, and institute big redistributionist governments to give them make-work jobs and transfer wealth to them from successful groups.

Which is what, very rationally and sensibly, they do.

Part 4c: The Cracker Factory
— John Derbyshire[2]

Neo-secessionists are all around us [...] and free speech gives them a cozy blanket of protection. Rick Perry insinuating Texas could secede rather than adhere to the federal healthcare law, Todd Palin belonging to a political association advocating Alaskan secession, and Sharron Angle talking about 'second amendment remedies' to handle disputes with federal authorities are all examples of dangerous secessionist rhetoric permeating through modern discourse. The media focuses our attention at Civil War reenactors and pick-up trucks with Confederate flags flying on them. But public figures are influenced as well, by academics who struggle to perpetuate a most dangerous brand of revisionism.
— Practically Historical[3]

African-Americans are the conscience of our country.
— Commenter 'surfed' at Walter Russell Mead's blog (edited for spelling)[4]

AMERICA's racial 'original sin' was foundational, dating back before the birth of the United States to the clearing of aboriginal peoples by European settlers, and—still more saliently—to the institution of chattel slavery. This is the Old Testament history of

2 John Derbyshire, "Who are We? — The 'Dissident Right'?", VDare, May 05, 2012, accessed August 04, 2022, https://vdare.com/articles/john-derbyshire-who-are-we-the-dissident-right.
3 Original link broken.
4 Original link broken.

American black-white relations, set down in a providential narrative of escape from bondage, in which factual documentation and moral exhortation are indissolubly fused. The combination of prolonged and intense social abuse in a pattern set by the Torah, recapitulating the primordial moral-political myth of the Western tradition, has installed the story of slavery and emancipation as the unsurpassable frame of the American historical experience: *let my people go*.

'Practically Historical' (cited above), quotes Lincoln on the Civil War:

> Yet, if God wills that it continue until all the wealth piled by the bondsman's two hundred and fifty years of unrequited toil shall be sunk, and until every drop of blood drawn with the lash shall be paid by another drawn with the sword, as was said three thousand years ago, so still it must be said "the judgments of the Lord are true and righteous altogether."

The New Testament of race in America was written in the 1960s, revising and specifying the template. The combination of the Civil Rights Movement, the 1965 Immigration and Nationality Act, and the Republican Southern Strategy (appealing to disaffected whites in the states of the old Confederacy) forged a partisan identification between Blacks and the Democratic Party that amounted to a liberal-progressive rebirth, setting the terms for partisan racial polarization that have endured—and even strengthened—over subsequent decades. For a progressive movement compromised by a history of systematic eugenicist racism, and a Democratic Party traditionally aligned with white southern obduracy and the Ku Klux Klan, the civil rights era presented an opportunity for atonement, ritual purification, and redemption.

Reciprocally, for American conservatism (and its increasingly directionless Republican Party vehicle), this progression spelt protracted death, for reasons that continue to elude it. The Idea of America was now inextricable from a vehement renunciation of the past, and even of the present, insofar as the past still shaped it. Only an 'ever more perfect union' could conform to it. At the most superficial level, the broad partisan implications of the new order were unmistakable in a country that was becoming ever more democratic, and ever less republican, with effective sovereignty nationally concentrated in the executive, and the moral urgency of activist government installed as a principle of faith. For what had already become the 'Old Right' there was no way out, or back, because the path backwards crossed the event horizon of the civil rights movement, into tracts of political impossibility whose ultimate meaning was slavery.

The left thrives on dialectics, the right perishes through them. Insofar as there is a pure logic of politics, it is that. One immediate consequence (repeatedly emphasized by Mencius Moldbug) is that progressivism has no enemies to the left. It recognizes only idealists, whose time has not yet come. Factional conflicts on the left are politically dynamic, celebrated for their motive potential. Conservatism, in contrast, is caught between a rock and a hard place: bludgeoned from the left by the juggernaut of post-constitutional statism, and agitated from 'the right' by inchoate tendencies which are both unassimilable (to the mainstream) and often mutually incompatible, ranging from extreme (Austro-libertarian) varieties of *laissez-faire* capitalist advocacy to strains of obstinate, theologically-grounded social traditionalism, ultra-nationalism, or white identity politics.

'The right' has no unity, actual or prospective, and thus has no definition symmetrical to that of the left. It is for this reason that political dialectics (a tautology) ratchets only in one direction, predictably, towards state expansion and an increasingly coercive substantial-egalitarian ideal. The right moves to the center, and the center moves to the left.

Regardless of mainstream conservative fantasies, liberal-progressive mastery of American providence has become uncontestable, dominated by a racial dialectic that absorbs unlimited contradiction, whilst positioning the Afro-American underclass as the incarnate critique of the existing social order, the criterion of emancipation, and the sole path to collective salvation. No alternative structure of historical intelligibility is politically tolerable, or even—strictly speaking—imaginable, since resistance to the narrative is un-American, anti-social, and (of course) racist, serving only to confirm the existence of systematic racial oppression through the symbolic violence manifested in its negation. To argue against it is already to prove it correct, by concretely demonstrating the same benighted forces of social retardation that are being verbally denied. By resisting the demand for orchestrated social re-education, knuckle-dragging 'bitter clingers' only show how much there still is to do.

Part 4c: The Cracker Factory

At its most abstract and all-encompassing, the liberal-progressive racial dialectic abolishes its outside, along with any possibility of principled consistency. It asserts—at one and the same time—that race does not exist, and that its socially-constructed pseudo-existence is an instrument of inter-racial violence. Racial recognition is both mandatory, and forbidden. Racial identities are meticulously catalogued for purposes of social remedy, hate crime detection, and disparate impact studies, targeting groups for 'positive discrimination', 'affirmative action', or 'diversity promotion' (to list these terms in their rough order of historical substitution), even as they are denounced as meaningless (by the United Nations, no less), and dismissed as malicious stereotypes, corresponding to nothing real. Extreme racial sensitivity and absolute racial desensitization are demanded simultaneously. Race is everything and nothing. There is no way out.

Conservatism is dialectically incompetent by definition, and so abjectly clueless that it imagines itself being able to exploit these contradictions, or—in its deluded formulation—*liberal cognitive dissonance*.[5] The conservatives who triumphantly point out such inconsistencies seem never to have skimmed the output of a contemporary humanities program, in which thick rafts of internally conflicted victimage are lovingly woven out of incompatible grievances, in order to exult in the radical progressive promise of their discordant lamentations. Inconsistency

---

5 John Derbyshire, "The Future of Elite Attitudes on Race," February 09, 2012, accessed August 04, 2022, https://www.johnderbyshire.com/Opinions/HumanSciences/racistelites.html.

is fuel for the Cathedral, demanding activist argumentation, and ever heightened realizations of unity. *Integrative public debate always moves things to the left*—that might not seem an especially difficult point to grasp, but to understand it is to expose the fundamental futility of mainstream conservatism, and that is in almost nobody's interest, so it will not be understood.

Conservatism is incapable of working dialectics, or simultaneous contradiction, but that does not prevent it from serving progress (on the contrary). Rather than celebrating the power of inconsistency, it stumbles through contradictions, decompressed, in succession, in the manner of a fossil exhibition, and a foil. After "standing athwart history, yelling 'Stop!'" during the Civil Rights Era, and thus banishing itself eternally to racial damnation, the conservative (and Republican) mainstream reversed course, seizing upon Martin Luther King Jr. as an integral part of its canon, and seeking to harmonize itself with "a dream deeply rooted in the American dream."

> I have a dream that one day this nation will rise up and live out the true meaning of its creed: "We hold these truths to be self-evident, that all men are created equal."
>
> I have a dream that one day on the red hills of Georgia the sons of former slaves and the sons of former slave owners will be able to sit down together at the table of brotherhood.
>
> I have a dream that one day even the state of Mississippi, a state sweltering with the heat of injustice, sweltering with the heat of oppression, will be transformed into an

> oasis of freedom and justice.
>
> I have a dream that my four little children will one day live in a nation where they will not be judged by the color of their skin but by the content of their character.[6]

Captivated by King's appeal to constitutional and biblical traditionalism, by his rejection of political violence, and by his uninhibited paeans to freedom, American conservatism gradually came to identify with his dream of racial reconciliation and race blindness, and to accept it as the true, providential meaning of its own most sacred documents. At least, this became the mainstream, public, conservative orthodoxy, even though it was consolidated far too late to neutralize suspicions of insincerity, failed almost entirely to convince the black demographic itself, and would remain open to escalating derision from the left for its empty formalism.

So compelling was King's restatement of the American Creed that, retrospectively, its triumph over the political mainstream seems simply inevitable. The further American conservatism departed from the Masonic rationalism of the founders, in the direction of biblical religiosity, the more indistinguishable its faith became from a Black American experience, mythically articulated through Exodus, in which the basic framework of history was an escape from bondage, borne towards a future in which "all of God's children—black men and white men,

---

[6] "Full Text of King's 'I Have a Dream' Speech," Chicago Tribune, January 31, 2013, accessed August 04, 2022, https://www.chicagotribune.com/nation-world/sns-mlk-ihaveadream-story.html.

Jews and Gentiles, Protestants and Catholics—will be able to join hands and sing in the words of the old Negro spiritual: 'Free at last! Free at last! Thank God Almighty, we are free at last!'"

The genius of King's message lay in its extraordinary power of integration. The flight of the Hebrews from Egypt, the American War of Independence, the abolition of chattel slavery in the wake of the American Civil War, and the aspirations of the civil rights era were mythically compressed into a single archetypal episode, perfectly consonant with the American Creed, and driven forwards not only by irresistible moral force, but even by divine decree. The measure of this integrative genius, however, is the complexity it masters. A century after the "joyous daybreak" of emancipation from slavery, King declares, "the Negro still is not free."

> One hundred years later, the life of the Negro is still sadly crippled by the manacles of segregation and the chains of discrimination. One hundred years later, the Negro lives on a lonely island of poverty in the midst of a vast ocean of material prosperity. One hundred years later, the Negro is still languished in the corners of American society and finds himself an exile in his own land.

The story of *Exodus* is exit, the War of Independence is exit, and the emancipation from slavery is exit, especially when this is exemplified by the Underground Railroad and the model of self-liberation, escape, or flight. To be 'manacled' by segregation, 'chained' by discrimination, trapped on a 'lonely island of poverty', or 'exiled' in one's 'own land', in contrast, has no relation to exit whatsoever, beyond that which spell-binding metaphor can achieve. There is no exit into social integration and acceptance, equitably distributed prosperity, public participation, or assimilation, but only an aspiration, or a dream, hostage to fact and fortune. As the left and the reactionary right were equally quick to notice, insofar as this dream ventures significantly beyond a right to formal equality and into the realm of substantial political remedy, it is one that the right has no right to.

In the immediate wake of the John Derbyshire affair, Jessica Valenti at *The Nation* blog makes the point clearly:

> [...] this isn't just about who has written what—it's about the intensely racist policies that are par for the conservative course. Some people would like to believe that racism is just the explicit, said-out-loud discrimination and hatred that is easily identifiable. It's not—it's also pushing xenophobic policies and supporting systemic inequality. After all, what's more impactful—a singular racist like Derbyshire or Arizona's immigration law? A column or voter suppression? Getting rid of one racist from one publication doesn't change the fact that the conservative agenda is one that disproportionately punishes and discriminates against people of color. So, I'm sorry, folks—you don't get to support structural inequality and then give yourself a pat on the back for not being overtly racist.[7]

7 Jessica Valenti, "Who Cares about John Derbyshire?",

The 'conservative agenda' cannot ever be dreamy (hopeful and inconsistent) enough to escape accusations of racism—that's intrinsic to the way the racial dialectic works. Policies broadly compatible with capitalistic development, oriented to the rewarding of low time-preference, and thus punishing impulsivity, will reliably have a disparate impact upon the least economically functional social groups. Of course, the dialectic demands that the racial aspect of this disparate impact can and must be strongly emphasized (for the purpose of condemning incentives to human capital formation as racist), and at the same time forcefully denied (in order to denounce *exactly the same observation* as racist stereotyping). Anyone who expects conservatives to navigate this double-bind with political agility and grace must somehow have missed the late 20th century. For instance, the conservatives at the *Washington Examiner*, noticing with alarm that:

> House Democrats received training this week on how to address the issue of race to defend government programs [...] The prepared content of a Tuesday presentation to the House Democratic Caucus and staff indicates that Democrats will seek to portray apparently neutral free-market rhetoric as being charged with racial bias, conscious or unconscious.[8]

There are no alternative versions of an ever more per-

April 09, 2012, accessed August 04, 2022, https://www.thenation.com/article/archive/who-cares-about-john-derbyshire/.
8 Original link broken.

fect union, because union is the alternative to alternatives. Searching for where the alternatives might once have been found, where liberty still meant *exit*, and where dialectics were dissolved in space, leads into a clown-house of horrors, fabricated as the shadow, or significant other, of the Cathedral. Since the right never had a unity of its own, it was given one. Call it the Cracker Factory.

When James C. Bennett, in *The Anglosphere Challenge*, sought to identify the principal cultural characteristics of the English-speaking world, the resulting list was generally familiar. It included, besides the language itself, common law traditions, individualism, comparatively high-levels of economic and technological openness, and distinctively emphatic reservations about centralized political power. Perhaps the most striking feature, however, was a marked cultural tendency to settle disagreements in space, rather than time, opting for territorial schism, separatism, independence, and flight, in place of revolutionary transformation within an integrated territory. When Anglophones disagree, they have often sought to dissociate in space. Instead of an integral resolution (regime change), they pursue a plural irresolution (through regime division), proliferating polities, localizing power, and diversifying systems of government. Even in its present, highly attenuated form, this anti-dialectical, de-synthesizing predisposition to social disaggregation finds expression in a stubborn, sussurous hostility to globalist political projects, and in a vestigial attraction to federalism (in its fissional sense).

Splitting, or fleeing, is all *exit*, and (non-recuperable) anti-dialectics. It is the basic well-spring of liberty within the Anglophone tradition. If the function of a Cracker Factory is to block off all the exits, there's only one place to build it—right here.

Like Hell, or Auschwitz, the Cracker Factory has a simple slogan inscribed upon its gate: *Escape is racist*. That is why the expression 'white flight'—which says exactly the same thing—has never been denounced for its political incorrectness, despite the fact that it draws upon an ethnic statistical generalization of the kind that would, in any other case, provoke paroxysms of outrage. 'White flight' is no more 'white' than low time-preference is, but this broad-brush insensitivity is deemed acceptable, because it structurally supports the Cracker Factory, and the indispensable confusion of ancient (or negative) liberty with original (racial) sin.

You absolutely, definitely, mustn't go there[9] ... so, of course, we will ... [next]

---

9 "League of the South," Southern Poverty Law Center, accessed August 04, 2022, https://www.splcenter.org/fighting-hate/extremist-files/group/league-south.

Part 4d: Odd Marriages

THE origins of the word 'cracker' as a term of ethnic derision are distant and obscure. It seems to have already circulated, as a slur targeting poor southern whites of predominantly Celtic ancestry, in the mid-18th century, derived perhaps from 'corn-cracker' or the Scots-Irish 'crack' (banter). The rich semantic complexion of the term, inextricable from the identification of elaborate racial, cultural, and class characteristics, is comparable to that of its unmentionable dusky cousin—"the 'N-'word"—and draws from the same well of generally recognized but forbidden truths.[1][2] In particular, and emphatically, it testifies to the *illicit truism* that people are more excited and animated by their differences than by their commonalities, 'clinging bitterly'—or at least tenaciously—to their non-uniformity, and obstinately resisting the universal categories of enlightened population management. Crackers are grit in

---

[1] Jonah Weiner, "'Niggas,' in Practice," Slate, June 12, 2012, accessed August 05, 2022, http://www.slate.com/articles/arts/music_box/2012/06/gwyneth_paltrow_and_niggas_in_paris_is_it_ever_ok_for_white_people_to_use_the_word_.html.
[2] Original link broken.

the clockwork of progress.

The most delectable features of the slur, however, are entirely fortuitous (or Qabbalistic). 'Crackers' break codes, safes, organic chemicals—sealed or bonded systems of all kinds—with eventual geopolitical implication. They anticipate a *crack-up*, schism or secession, confirming their association with the anathematized disintegrative undercurrent of Anglophone history. No surprise, then—despite the linguistic jumps and glitching—that the figure of the recalcitrant cracker evokes a still-unpacified South, insubordinate to the manifest destiny of Union. This returns it, by short-circuit, to the most problematic depths of its meaning.

Contradictions demand resolution, but *cracks* can continue to widen, deepen, and spread. According to the cracker ethos, when things can fall apart—it's OK. There's no need to reach agreement, when it's possible to split. This *cussedness*, pursued to its limit, tends to a hill-billy stereotype set in a shack or rusting trailer at the end of an Appalachian mountain path, where all economic transactions are conducted in cash (or moonshine), interactions with government agents are conducted across the barrel of a loaded shotgun, and timeless anti-political wisdom is summed in the don't-tread-on-me reflex: "Get off my porch." Naturally, this disdain for integrative debate (dialectics) is coded within the mainstream of Anglocentric global history—which is to say, Yankee evangelical Puritanism—as a deficiency not only of cultural sophistication, but also of basic intelligence, and even the most scrupulous adherent of social constructivist righteousness immediately reverts to hard-hereditarian psychometrics when confronted by cracker obstreperousness. To those for whom a broad trend of socio-political progress seems like a simple, incontestable fact, the refusal to recognize anything of the kind is perceived as clear evidence of retardation.

Since stereotypes generally have high statistical truth-value, it's more than possible that crackers are clustered heavily on the left of the white IQ bell-curve, concentrated there by generations of dysgenic pressure. If, as Charles Murray argues, the efficiency of meritocratic selection within American society has steadily risen and conspired with assortative mating to transform class differences into genetic castes, it would be passing strange if the cracker stratum were to be characterized by conspicuous cognitive elevation. Yet some awkwardly intriguing questions intervene at this point, as long as one diligently pursues the stereotype. Assortative mating? How can that work, when crackers marry their cousins? Oh yes, there's *that*. Drawing on population groups beyond the north-western Hajnal Line, traditional cracker kinship patterns are notably atypical of the exogamous Anglo (WASP) norm.[3][4]

The tireless 'hbdchick' is the crucial resource on this topic.[5] Over the course of a truly monumental series of blog posts,[6] she employs Hamiltonian[7] conceptu-

---

3 "Medieval Manorialism and the Hajnal Line," hbdchick, June 06, 2012, accessed August 05, 2022, https://hbdchick.wordpress.com/2012/02/06/medieval-manoralism-and-the-hajnal-line/.
4 Original link broken.
5 See https://hbdchick.wordpress.com/.
6 Original link broken.
7 "W. D. Hamilton," Wikipedia, accessed August 05,

al tools to investigate the borderland where nature and culture intersect, comprising kinship structures, the differentiations they require in the calculus of inclusive fitness, and the distinctive ethnic profiles in the evolutionary psychology of altruism that result. In particular, she directs attention to the abnormality of (North-West) European history, where obligatory exogamy—through rigorous proscription of cousin marriage—has prevailed for 1,600 years. This distinctive orientation towards outbreeding, she suggests, plausibly accounts for a variety of bio-cultural peculiarities, the most historically significant of which is a unique pre-eminence of reciprocal (over familial) altruism, as indicated by emphatic individualism, nuclear families, an affinity with 'corporate' (kinship-free) institutions, highly-developed contractual relationships among strangers, relatively low levels of nepotism/corruption, and robust forms of social cohesion independent of tribal bonds.

Inbreeding, in contrast, creates a selective environment favoring tribal collectivism, extended systems of family loyalty and honor, distrust of non-relatives and impersonal institutions, and—in general—those 'clannish' traits which mesh uncomfortably with the leading values of (Eurocentric) modernity, and are thus denounced for their primitive 'xenophobia' and 'corruption'. Clannish values, of course, are bred in clans, such as those populating Britain's Celtic fringe and borderlands, where cousin marriage persisted, along with its associated socio-economic and cultural forms, especially herding (rather than farming), and a disposition towards extreme, vendetta-style

2022, https://en.wikipedia.org/wiki/W._D._Hamilton.

violence.[8]

This analysis introduces the central paradox of 'white identity', since the specifically European ethnic traits that have structured the moral order of modernity, slanting it away from tribalism and towards reciprocal altruism, are inseparable from a unique heritage of outbreeding that is intrinsically corrosive of ethnocentric solidarity. In other words: it is almost exactly weak ethnic groupishness that makes a group ethnically modernistic, competent at 'corporate' (non-familial) institution building, and thus objectively privileged/advantaged within the dynamic of modernity.

This paradox is most fully expressed in the radical forms of European ethnocentric revivalism exemplified by paleo- and neo-Nazism, confounding its proponents and antagonists alike. When exceptionally advanced 'race-treachery' is your quintessential racial feature, the opportunity for viable ethno-supremacist politics disappears into a logical abyss—even if occasions for large-scale trouble-making no doubt remain. Admittedly, a Nazi, by definition, is willing (and eager) to sacrifice modernity upon the altar of racial purity, but this is either not to understand, or to tragically affirm, the inevitable consequence—which is to be out-modernized (and thus defeated). Identity politics is for losers, inherently and unalterably, due to an essentially parasitical character that only works from the left. Because inbreeding systematically contra-indicates for modern power, racial *Übermenschen* make no real sense.

8 "'Culture' of Honour," hbdchick, January 27, 2012, accessed August 05, 2022, https://hbdchick.wordpress.com/2012/01/27/culture-of-honor/.

In any case, however endlessly fascinating Nazis may be, they are not any kind of reliable key to the history or direction of cracker culture, beyond setting a logical limit to the programmatic construction and usage of white identity politics.[9] Tattooing swastikas on their foreheads does nothing to change that. (Hatfields vs McCoys is more Pushtun than Teuton.)[10]

The conjunction taking place in the Cracker Factory is quite different, and far more perplexing, entangling the urbane, cosmopolitan advocates of hyper-contractarian marketization with romantic traditionalists, ethno-particularists, and nostalgics of the 'Lost Cause'. It is first necessary to understand this entanglement in its full, mind-melting weirdness, before exploring its lessons. For that, some semi-random stripped-down data-points might be helpful:

- The Mises Institute was founded in Auburn, Alabama.[11]

- Ron Paul newsletters from the 1980s contain remarks of a decidedly Derbyshirean hue.[12]

- Derbyshire hearts Ron Paul.[13]

---

9 Grady McWhiney, *Cracker Culture: Celtic Ways in the Old South* (Alabama: The University of Alabama Press, 1989).

10 "Hatfields and McCoys," hbdchick, May 31, 2012, accessed August 05, 2022, https://hbdchick.wordpress.com/2012/05/31/hatfields-and-mccoys/.

11 See https://mises.org/about-mises.

12 Original link broken.

13 John Derbyshire, "Liberty! Liberty!", December 20, 2007, accessed August 05, 2022, https://johnderbyshire.

Part 4d: Odd Marriages

- Murray Rothbard has written in defense of HBD.[14]
- lewrockwell.com contributors include Thomas J. DiLorenzo and Thomas Woods.[15] [16]
- Tom Palmer doesn't heart Lew Rockwell or Hans-Hermann Hoppe because "Together They Have Opened the Gates of Hell and Welcomed the Most Extreme Right-Wing Racists, Nationalists, and Assorted Cranks".[17]
- Libertarians/constitutionalists account for 20% of the SPLC 'Radical Right' watch list (Chuck Baldwin, Michael Boldin, Tom DeWeese, Alex Jones, Cliff Kincaid, and Elmer Stewart Rhodes).[18]

…perhaps that's enough to be going on with (al-

---

com/Opinions/USPolitics/libertyliberty.html.

14 Murray Rothbard, "Egalitarianism as a Revolt Against Nature," LewRockwell.com, accessed August 05, 2022, https://www.lewrockwell.com/1970/01/murray-n-rothbard/were-not-equal/.

15 See https://www.lewrockwell.com/author/thomas-dilorenzo/.

16 See https://www.lewrockwell.com/author/thomas-woods/.

17 Tom G. Palmer, "Hans-Hermann Hoppe and the German Extremist Nationalist Right," July 01, 2005, accessed August 05, 2022, http://tomgpalmer.com/2005/07/01/hans-hermann-hoppe-and-the-german-extremist-nationalist-right/.

18 "30 New Activists Heading up the Radical Right," May 26, 2012, accessed August 05, 2022, https://www.splcenter.org/fighting-hate/intelligence-report/2012/30-new-activists-heading-radical-right.

though there's plenty more within easy reach). These points have been selected, questionably, crudely, and prejudicially, to lend impressionistic support to a single basic thesis: *fundamental socio-historical forces are crackerizing libertarianism.*

If the tentative research conclusions drawn by hbdchick are accepted as a frame, the oddity of this marriage between libertarian and neo-confederate themes is immediately apparent. When positioned on a bio-cultural axis, defined by degrees of outbreeding, the absence of overlap—or even proximity—is dramatically exposed. One pole is occupied by a radically individualistic doctrine, focused near-exclusively upon mutable networks of voluntary interchange of an economic type (and notoriously insensitive to the very existence of non-negotiable social bonds). Close to the other pole lies a rich culture of local attachment, extended family, honor, contempt for commercial values, and distrust of strangers. The distilled rationality of fluid capitalism is juxtaposed to traditional hierarchy and non-alienable value. The absolute prioritization of *exit* is jumbled amongst folkways from which no exit is even imaginable.

Stapling the two together, however, is a simple, ever more irresistible conclusion: liberty has no future in the Anglophone world outside the prospect of secession. The coming crack-up is the only way out.

Part 4e: Cross-Coded History

Democracy is the opposite of freedom, almost inherent to the democratic process is that it tends towards less liberty instead of more, and democracy is not something to be fixed. Democracy is inherently broken, just like socialism. The only way to fix it is to break it up.
—Frank Karsten[1]

Historian (mainly of science) Doug Fosnow called for the USA's "red" counties to secede from the "blue" ones, forming a new federation. This was greeted with much skepticism by the audience, who noted that the "red" federation would get practically no seacoast. Did Doug really think such a secession was likely to happen? No, he admitted cheerfully, but anything would be better than the race war he does think is likely to happen, and it is intellectuals' duty to come up with less horrific possibilities.

---

1 Frank Karsten, "Democracy Can't be Fixed. It's Inherently Broken." Against Politics, March 30, 2012, accessed August 05, 2022, https://web.archive.org/web/20170627002622/http://againstpolitics.com:80/2012/03/30/democracy-cant-be-fixed-its-inherently-broken/.

– John Derbyshire[2]

Thus, rather than by means of a top-down reform, under the current conditions, one's strategy must be one of a bottom-up revolution. At first, the realization of this insight would seem to make the task of a liberal-libertarian social revolution impossible, for does this not imply that one would have to persuade a majority of the public to vote for the abolition of democracy and an end to all taxes and legislation? And is this not sheer fantasy, given that the masses are always dull and indolent, and even more so given that democracy, as explained above, promotes moral and intellectual degeneration? How in the world can anyone expect that a majority of an increasingly degenerate people accustomed to the "right" to vote should ever voluntarily renounce the opportunity of looting other people's property? Put this way, one must admit that the prospect of a social revolution must indeed be regarded as virtually nil. Rather, it is only on second thought, upon regarding secession as an integral part of any bottom-up strategy, that the task of a liberal-libertarian revolution appears less than impossible, even if it still remains a daunting one.

– Hans-Hermann Hoppe[3]

---

2 John Derbyshire, "Partying with the Right Side on the Left Coast," Taki's Magazine, June 28, 2012, accessed August 05, 2022, https://www.takimag.com/article/partying_with_the_right_side_on_the_left_coast_john_derbyshire/.

3 Hans-Hermann Hoppe, "The Impossibility of Limited Government and the Prospects for a Second American Revolution," in *Reassessing the Presidency*, John V. Denson

Part 4e: Cross-Coded History

CONCEIVED generically, modernity is a social condition defined by an integral trend, summarized as sustained economic growth rates that exceed population increases, and thus mark an escape from normal history, caged within the Malthusian trap. When, in the interest of dispassionate appraisal, analysis is restricted to the terms of this basic quantitative pattern, it supports sub-division into the (growth) positive and negative components of the trend: techno-industrial (scientific and commercial) contributions to accelerating development on the one hand, and socio-political counter-tendencies towards the capture of economic product by democratically empowered rent-seeking special interests on the other (demosclerosis).[4] What classical liberalism gives (industrial revolution) mature liberalism takes away (via the cancerous entitlement state). In abstract geometry, it describes an S-curve of self-limiting runaway. As a drama of liberation, it is a broken promise.

Conceived particularly, as a singularity, or real *thing*, modernity has ethno-geographical characteristics that complicate and qualify its mathematical purity. It came from somewhere, imposed itself more widely, and brought the world's various peoples into an extraordinary range of novel relations. These relations were characteristically 'modern' if they involved an overflowing of previous Malthusian limits, enabling capital accumulation, and initiating new demographic trends, but they conjoined concrete

(Auburn: Mises Institute, 2001), pp. 667–696.
4 Jonathan Rauch, "Demosclerosis," September 05, 1992, accessed August 05, 2022, https://www.jonathanrauch.com/jrauch_articles/demosclerosis_the_original_article/.

groups rather than abstract economic functions. At least in appearance, therefore, modernity was something done by people of a certain kind with, and not uncommonly to (or even against), other people, who were conspicuously unlike them. By the time it was faltering on the fading slope of the S-curve, in the early 20th century, resistance to its generic features ('capitalistic alienation') had become almost entirely indistinguishable from opposition to its particularity ('European imperialism' and 'white supremacy'). As an inevitable consequence, the modernistic self-consciousness of the system's ethno-geographical core slid towards racial panic, in a process that was only arrested by the rise and immolation of the Third Reich.[5][6][7]

Given modernity's inherent trend to degeneration or self-cancellation, three broad prospects open. These are not strictly exclusive, and are therefore not true alternatives, but for schematic purposes it is helpful to present them as such.

1. Modernity 2.0. Global modernization is re-invigorated from a new ethno-geographical core, liberated from the degenerate struc-

---

[5] Kerry Bolton, "Ezra Pound," accessed August 05, 2022, http://library.flawlesslogic.com/pound.htm.

[6] James B. Lubinskas, "A Warning from the Past: Lothrop Stoddard and *The Rising Tide of Color*," The Occidental Quarterly, March 29, 2010, accessed August 05, 2022, https://web.archive.org/web/20170705234006/http://www.toqonline.com/blog/lothrop-stoddard-and-the-rising-tide-of-color/.

[7] "H. P. Lovecraft," Great Minds on Race, October 02, 2011, accessed August 05, 2022, https://greatmindsonrace.wordpress.com/2011/10/02/h-p-lovecraft/.

tures of its Eurocentric predecessor, but no doubt confronting long range trends of an equally mortuary character. This is by far the most encouraging and plausible scenario (from a pro-modernist perspective), and if China remains even approximately on its current track it will be assuredly realized. (India, sadly, seems to be too far gone in its native version of demosclerosis to seriously compete.)

2. Postmodernity. Amounting essentially to a new dark age, in which Malthusian limits brutally re-impose themselves, this scenario assumes that Modernity 1.0 has so radically globalized its own morbidity that the entire future of the world collapses around it. If the Cathedral 'wins' this is what we have coming.

3. Western Renaissance. To be reborn it is first necessary to die, so the harder the 'hard reboot' the better. Comprehensive crisis and disintegration offers the best odds (most realistically as a sub-theme of option #1).

Because competition is good, a pinch of Western Renaissance would spice things up, even if—as is overwhelmingly probable—Modernity 2.0 is the world's principal highway to the future. That depends upon the West stopping and reversing pretty much everything it has been doing for over a century, excepting only scientific, technological, and business innovation. It is advisable to maintain rhetorical discipline within a strictly hypothetical mode, because the possibility of any of these things is deeply colored by incredibility:

1. Replacement of representational democracy by constitutional republicanism (or still more extreme anti-political governmental mechanisms).[8]

2. Massive downsizing of government and its rigorous confinement to core functions (at most).[9]

3. Restoration of hard money (precious metal coins and bullion deposit notes) and abolition of central banking.

4. Dismantling of state monetary and fiscal discretion, thus abolishing practical macroeconomics and liberating the autonomous (or 'catallactic') economy. (This point is redundant, since it follows rigorously from 2 & 3 above, but it's the real prize, so worth emphasizing.)

There's more—which is to say, less politics—but it's already absolutely clear that none of this is going to happen short of an existential civilizational cataclysm. Asking politicians to limit their own powers is a non-starter, but nothing less heads even remotely in the right direction. This, however, isn't even the widest or deepest problem.

Democracy might begin as a defensible procedur-

---

[8] Jacob Lyles, "Rampant Moldbuggery," The Distributed Republic, December 18, 2008, accessed August 05, 2022, https://distributedrepublic.net/archives/2008/12/18/rampant-moldbuggery/.

[9] David Friedman, *Machinery of Freedom: Guide to a Radical Capitalism* (Chicago: Open Court Publishing, 2000).

al mechanism for limiting government power, but it quickly and inexorably develops into something quite different: a culture of systematic thievery. As soon as politicians have learnt to buy political support from the 'public purse', and conditioned electorates to embrace looting and bribery, the democratic process reduces itself to the formation of (Mancur Olson's) 'distributional coalitions'—electoral majorities mortared together by common interest in a collectively advantageous pattern of theft. Worse still, since people are, on average, not very bright, the scale of depredation available to the political establishment far exceeds even the demented sacking that is open to public scrutiny. Looting the future, through currency debauchment, debt accumulation, growth destruction, and techno-industrial retardation is especially easy to conceal, and thus reliably popular. Democracy is essentially tragic because it provides the populace with a weapon to destroy itself, one that is always eagerly seized, and used. Nobody ever says 'no' to free stuff. Scarcely anybody even sees that there is no free stuff. Utter cultural ruination is the necessary conclusion.

Within the final phase of Modernity 1.0, American history becomes the master narrative of the world. It is there that the great Abrahamic cultural conveyor culminates in the secularized neo-puritanism of the Cathedral, as it establishes the New Jerusalem in Washington DC. The apparatus of Messianic-revolutionary purpose is consolidated in the evangelical state, which is authorized by any means necessary to install a new world order of universal fraternity, in the name of equality, human rights, social justice, and—above all—*democracy*. The absolute moral confidence of the Cathedral underwrites the enthusiastic pursuit of unrestrained centralized power, optimally unlimited in its intensive penetration and its extensive scope.

With an irony altogether hidden from the witch-burners' spawn themselves, the ascent of this squinting cohort of grim moral fanatics to previously unscaled heights of global power coincides with the descent of mass-democracy to previously unimagined depths of gluttonous corruption. Every five years America steals itself from itself again, and fences itself back in exchange for political support. *This democracy thing is easy—you just vote for the guy who promises you the most stuff. An idiot could do it.* Actually, it likes idiots, treats them with apparent kindness, and does everything it can to manufacture more of them.

Democracy's relentless trend to degeneration presents an implicit case for reaction. Since every major threshold of socio-political 'progress' has ratcheted Western civilization towards comprehensive ruin, a retracing of its steps suggests a reversion from the society of pillage to an older order of self-reliance, honest industry and exchange, pre-propagandistic learning, and civic self-organization. The attractions of this reactionary vision are evidenced by the vogue for 18th century attire, symbols, and constitutional documents among the substantial (Tea Party) minority who clearly see the disastrous course of American political history.

Has the 'race' alarm sounded in your head yet? It would be amazing if it hadn't. Stagger back in imagination before 2008, and the fraught whisper of conscience is already questioning your prejudices against

Part 4e: Cross-Coded History

Kenyan revolutionaries and black Marxist professors. Remain in reverse until the Great Society/Civil Rights era and the warnings reach hysterical pitch. It's perfectly obvious by this point that American political history has progressed along twin, interlocking tracks, corresponding to the *capacity* and the *legitimation* of the state. To cast doubt upon its scale and scope is to simultaneously dispute the sanctity of its purpose, and the moral-spiritual necessity that it command whatever resources, and impose whatever legal restraints, may be required to effectively fulfill it. More specifically, to recoil from the magnitude of Leviathan is to demonstrate insensitivity to the immensity—indeed, near infinity—of inherited racial guilt, and the sole surviving categorical imperative of senescent modernity—government needs to *do more*. The possibility, indeed near certainty, that the pathological consequences of chronic government activism have long ago supplanted the problems they originally targeted, is a contention so utterly maladapted to the epoch of democratic religion that its practical insignificance is assured.

Even on the left, it would be extraordinary to find many who genuinely believe, after sustained reflection, that the primary driver of government expansion and centralization has been the burning desire *to do good* (not that intentions matter). Yet, as the twin tracks cross, such is the electric jolt of moral drama, leaping the gap from racial Golgotha to intrusive Leviathan, that skepticism is suspended, and the great progressive myth installed. *The alternative to more government, doing ever more, was to stand there, negligently, whilst they lynched another Negro.* This proposition contains the entire essential content of American progressive education.

The twin historical tracks of state capability and purpose can be conceived as a translation protocol, enabling any recommended restraint upon government power to be 'decoded' as malign obstruction of racial justice. This system of substitutions functions so smoothly that it provides an entire vocabulary of (bipartisan) 'code-words' or 'dog-whistles'—'welfare', 'freedom of association', 'states rights'—ensuring that any intelligible utterance on the Principal (left-right) Political Dimension occupies a double registry, semi-saturated by racial evocations. Reactionary regression smells of strange fruit.

…and that is before backing out of the calamitous 20th century. It was not the Civil Rights Era, but the 'American Civil War' (in the terms of the victors) or 'War between the States' (in those of the vanquished) that first indissolubly cross-coded the practical question of Leviathan with (black/white) racial dialectics, laying down the central junction yard of subsequent political antagonism and rhetoric. The indispensable primary step in comprehending this fatality snakes along an awkward diagonal between mainstream statist and revisionist accounts, because the conflagration that consumed the American nation in the early 1860s was wholly but non-exclusively about emancipation from slavery and about states' rights,[10] with neither 'cause' reducible to the other, or sufficient to suppress the war's enduring

---

10 Mike Crane, "What is States' Rights," League of the South, 15 August, 2017, accessed August 05, 2022, https://web.archive.org/web/20170815125928/http://dixienet.org/rights/2013/what_is_states_rights_part1.php.

ambiguities. Whilst there are any number of 'liberals' happy to celebrate the consolidation of centralized government power in the triumphant Union, and, symmetrically, a (far smaller) number of neo-confederate apologists for the institution of chattel slavery in the southern states, neither of these unconflicted stances capture the dynamic cultural legacy of a *war across the codes*.

The war is a knot. By practically dissociating liberty into *emancipation* and *independence*, then hurling each against the other in a half-decade of carnage, blue against gray, it was settled that freedom would be broken on the battlefield, whatever the outcome of the conflict. Union victory determined that the emancipatory sense of liberty would prevail, not only in America, but throughout the world, and the eventual reign of the Cathedral was assured. Nevertheless, the crushing of American's second war of secession made a mockery of the first. If the institution of slavery de-legitimated a war of independence, what survived of 1776? The moral coherence of the Union cause required that the founders were reconceived as politically illegitimate white patriarchal slave-owners, and American history combusted in progressive education and the culture wars.

If independence is the ideology of slave-holders, emancipation requires the programmatic destruction of independence. Within a cross-coded history, the realization of freedom is indistinguishable from its abolition.

Part 4f: Approaching the Bionic Horizon

It's time to bring this long digression to a conclusion, by reaching out impatiently towards the end. The basic theme has been mind control, or thought-suppression, as demonstrated by the Media-Academic complex that dominates contemporary Western societies, and which Mencius Moldbug names the Cathedral. When things are squashed they rarely disappear. Instead, they are displaced, fleeing into sheltering shadows, and sometimes turning into monsters. Today, as the suppressive orthodoxy of the Cathedral comes unstrung, in various ways, and numerous senses, a time of monsters is approaching.

The central dogma of the Cathedral has been formalized as the Standard Social Scientific Model (SSSM) or 'blank slate theory'.[1][2] It is the belief,

1 Leda Cosmides & John Tooby, "Evolutionary Psychology: A Primer," accessed August 05, 2022, http://www.sscnet.ucla.edu/comm/steen/cogweb/ep/EP-primer.html.
2 Richard Lynn, "John Harvey's Race and Equality: The 'Standard Social Science Model' is W-R-O-N-G," Vdare, April 04, 2012, accessed August 05, 2022, https://vdare.com/articles/john-harvey-s-race-and-equality-the-

completed in its essentials by the anthropology of Franz Boas, that every legitimate question about mankind is restricted to the sphere of culture.[3] Nature permits *that* 'man' is, but never determines *what* man is. Questions directed towards natural characteristics and variations between humans are themselves properly understood as cultural peculiarities, or even pathologies. Failures of 'nurture' are the only thing we are allowed to see.

Because the Cathedral has a consistent ideological orientation, and sifts its enemies accordingly, comparatively detached scientific appraisal of the SSSM easily veers into raw antagonism. As Simon Blackburn remarks (in a thoughtful review of Steven Pinker's *The Blank Slate*), "The dichotomy between nature and nurture rapidly acquires political and emotional implications. To put it crudely, the right likes genes and the left likes culture [...]"[4]

At the limit of reciprocal loathing, hereditary determinism confronts social constructivism, with each committed to a radically pared-back model of causality. *Either* nature expresses itself as culture, or culture expresses itself in its images ('constructions') of nature. Both of these positions are trapped at opposite sides of an incomplete circuit, structurally blinded to *the culture of practical naturalism*, which is to say: the techno-scientific/industrial manipulation of the world.

Acquiring knowledge and using tools is a single dynamic circuit, producing techno-science as an in-

standard-social-science-model-is-w-r-o-n-g.
3 Herbert Lewis, "The Passion of Franz Boas," *American Anthropologist* 103, no. 2 (2001): pp. 447–467.
4 Original link broken.

tegral system, without real divisibility into theoretical and practical aspects. Science develops in loops, through experimental *technique* and the production of ever more sophisticated instrumentation, whilst embedded within a broader industrial process. Its advance is the improvement of a machine. This intrinsically technological character of (modern) science demonstrates the *efficiency* of culture as a complex natural force. It neither expresses a pre-existing natural circumstance, nor does it merely construct social representations. Instead, nature and culture compose a dynamic circuit, at the edge of nature, where fate is decided.

According to the self-reinforcing presupposition of modernization, to be understood is to be modifiable. It is to be expected, therefore, that biology and medicine co-evolve. The same historical dynamic that comprehensively subverts the SSSM through inundating waves of scientific discovery simultaneously volatilizes human biological identity through biotechnology. There is no essential difference between learning what we *really are* and re-defining ourselves as technological contingencies, or *technoplastic* beings, susceptible to precise, scientifically-informed transformations. 'Humanity' becomes intelligible as it is subsumed into the technosphere, where information processing of the genome—for instance—brings reading and editing into perfect coincidence.

To describe this circuit, as it consumes the human species, is to define our *bionic horizon*: the threshold of conclusive nature-culture fusion at which a population becomes indistinguishable from its technology. This is neither hereditarian determinism, nor social constructivism, but it is what both

Part 4f: Approaching the Bionic Horizon

would have referred to, had they indicated anything real. It is a syndrome vividly anticipated by Octavia Butler, whose Xenogenesis trilogy is devoted to the examination of a population beyond the bionic horizon.[5] Her Oankali 'gene traders' have no identity separable from the biotechnological program that they perpetually implement upon themselves, as they commercially acquire, industrially produce, and sexually reproduce their population within a single, integral process. Between what the Oankali are, and the way they live, or behave, there is no firm difference. Because they make themselves, their nature is their culture and (of course) reciprocally. What they *are* is exactly what they *do*.

Religious traditionalists of the Western Orthosphere are right to identify the looming bionic horizon with a (negative) theological event. Techno-scientific auto-production specifically supplants the fixed and sacralized essence of man as a created being, amidst the greatest upheaval in the natural order since the emergence of eukaryotic life, half a billion years ago. It is not merely an evolutionary event, but the threshold of a new *evolutionary phase*. John H. Campbell heralds the emergence of *Homo autocatalyticus*, whilst arguing: "In point of fact, it is hard to imagine how a system of inheritance could be more ideal for engineering than ours is."[6]

John H. Campbell?—a prophet of monstrosity, and the perfect excuse for a monster quote:

---

5 Joan Slonczewski, "Octavia Butler: A Biologist's Response," accessed August 05, 2022, https://biology.kenyon.edu/slonc/butler1997/butler.htm#Xeno.
6 [Link broken.]

Biologists suspect that new forms evolve rapidly from very tiny outgroups of individuals (perhaps even a single fertilized female, Mayr, 1942) at the fringe of an existing species. There the stress of an all but uninhabitable environment, forced inbreeding among isolated family members, "introgression" of foreign genes from neighboring species, lack of other members of the species to compete against or whatever, promotes a major reorganization of the genomic program, possibly from modest change in gene structure. Nearly all of these transmogrified fragments of species die out, but an occasional one is fortunate enough to fit a new viable niche. It prospers and expands into a new species. Its conversion into a statistically constrained gene pool then stabilizes the species from further evolutionary change. Established species are far more notable for their stasis than change. Even throwing off a new daughter species does not seem to change an existing species. No one denies that species can gradually transform and do so to various extents, but this so-called "anagenesis" is relatively unimportant compared to geologically-sudden major saltation in the generation of novelty.

Three implications are important.

1. Most evolutionary change is associated with the origin of new species.

2. Several modes of evolution may operate simultaneously. In this case the most effective dominates the process.

3. Tiny minorities of individuals do

most of the evolving instead of the species as a whole.

A second important characteristic of evolution is self-reference (Campbell, 1982). The Cartesian cartoon of an autonomous external "environment" dictating the form of a species like a cookie cutter cutting stencils from sheets of dough is dead, dead wrong. The species molds its environment as profoundly as the environment "evolves" the species. In particular, the organisms cause the limiting conditions of the environment over which they compete. Therefore the genes play two roles in evolution. They are the targets of natural selection and they also ultimately induce and determine the selection pressures that act upon them. This circular causality overwhelms the mechanical character of evolution. Evolution is dominated by feedback of the evolved activities of organisms on their evolution.

The third seminal realization is that evolution extends past the change in organisms as products of evolution to change in the process itself. Evolution evolves (Jantsch, 1976; Balsh, 1989; Dawkins, 1989; Campbell, 1993). Evolutionists know this fact but have never accorded the fact the importance that it deserves because it is incommensurate with Darwinism. Darwinists, and especially modern neodarwinists, equate evolution to the operation of a simple logical principle, one that is prior to biology: Evolution is merely the Darwinian principle of natural selection in action, and this is what the science of evolution is about. Since principles cannot change with time or circumstances, evolution must be fundamentally static.

Of course, biological evolution is not like this at all. It is an actual complex process, not a principle. The way that it takes place can, and indisputably does, change with time. This is of utmost importance because the process of evolution advances as it proceeds (Campbell, 1986). Preliving matter in the earth's primordial soup was able to evolve only by subdarwinian "chemical" mechanisms. Once these puny processes created gene molecules with information for their self-replication then evolution was able to engage natural selection. Evolution then wrapped the self-replicating genomes within self-replicating organisms to control the way that life would respond to the winds of selection from the environment. Later, by creating multicellular organisms, evolution gained access to morphological change as an alternative to slower and less versatile biochemical evolution. Changes in the instructions in developmental programs replaced changes in enzyme catalysts. Nervous systems opened the way for still faster and more potent behavioral, social and cultural evolution. Finally, these higher modes produced the prerequisite organization for rational, purposeful evolution, guided and propelled by goal-directed minds. Each of these steps represented a new emergent level of evolutionary capability.

Thus, there are two distinct, but interwoven, evolutionary processes. I call them

Part 4f: Approaching the Bionic Horizon

"adaptive evolution" and "generative evolution." The former is familiar Darwinian modification of organisms to enhance their survival and reproductive success. Generative evolution is entirely different. It is the change in a process instead of structure. Moreover, that process is ontological. Evolution literally means "to unfold" and what is unfolding is the capacity to evolve. Higher animals have become increasingly adept at evolving. In contrast, they are not the least bit fitter than their ancestors or the lowest form of microbe. Every species today has had exactly the same track record of survival; on average, every higher organism alive today still will leave only two offspring, as was the case a hundred million years ago, and modern species are as likely to go extinct as were those in the past. Species cannot become fitter and fitter because reproductive success is not a cumulative parameter.

For racial nationalists, concerned that their grandchildren should look like them, Campbell is the abyss. Miscegenation doesn't get close to the issue. *Think face tentacles.*

Campbell is also a secessionist, although entirely undistracted by the concerns of identity politics (racial purity) or traditional cognitive elitism (eugenics). Approaching the bionic horizon, secessionism takes on an altogether wilder and more monstrous bearing—towards *speciation*. The folks at euvolution capture the scenario well:

> Reasoning that the majority of humankind

> will not voluntarily accept qualitative population-management policies, Campbell points out that any attempt to raise the IQ of the whole human race would be tediously slow. He further points out that the general thrust of early eugenics was not so much species improvement as the prevention of decline. Campbell's eugenics, therefore, advocates the abandonment of Homo sapiens as a 'relic' or 'living fossil' and the application of genetic technologies to intrude upon the genome, probably writing novel genes from scratch using a DNA synthesizer. Such eugenics would be practiced by elite groups, whose achievements would so quickly and radically outdistance the usual tempo of evolution that within ten generation [sic] the new groups will have advanced beyond our current form to the same degree that we transcend apes.[7]

When seen from the bionic horizon, whatever emerges from the dialectics of racial terror remains trapped in trivialities. It's time to move on.

---

7 "Radical Intervention," Euvolution, accessed August 05, 2022, https://www.euvolution.com/eugenics/radical_intervention.html.

Studies in Reaction Series:

I	Jonathan Bowden	*Why I Am Not a Liberal*
II	Thomas Carlyle	*The Present Time*
III	George Fitzhugh	*Sociology for the South*
IV	Henry Sumner Maine	*Popular Government*
V	Sophocles	*Ajax*
VI	Numa Denis Fustel de Coulanges	*The Ancient Family*
VII		*Havamal and Norse Proverbs*
VIII	Joseph de Maistre	*On the Spanish Inquisition*
IX	Nick Land	*The Dark Enlightenment*
X	Hans Freyer	*Revolution from the Right*
XI	Edgar Jung	*On the Threshold of a New Era*
XII	Oswald Spengler	*Pessimism and Other Political Essays*
XIII	François-René, vicomte de Chateaubriand	*Selected Writings*
XIV	Arthur Moeller van den Bruck	*Fatherland and Motherland*

www.ingramcontent.com/pod-product-compliance
Lightning Source LLC
Chambersburg PA
CBHW030039100526
44590CB00011B/267